Circles, PSHE and Citizensnip

A Lucky Duck Book

Marilyn Tew is a freelance consultant, trainer and facilitator and is currently working with Antidote to shape learning environments that offer young people the best possible opportunity to achieve and make a positive contribution. She has worked with schools nationally and internationally across all phases and recently spent a year working as an Assistant Head Teacher in a large secondary school in the UK. For the past eight years, she has had a special interest in the relevance of group work, emotional literacy and Circle Time to PSHE.

Mary Read was Assistant Head Teacher at Hayesfield School in Bath for fifteen years. She has taught for over twenty-five years, developing a particular interest in the holistic education of children, enabling students to live and learn with good emotional and physical health. Specialising in Philosophy and Beliefs and PSHE from ages 11 to 18 she has taught through circles for many years. She is currently continuing to teach part-time at Hayesfield School as well as writing and working as a trainer nationally.

Hilary Potter has direct and recent experience of teaching and training across a range of educational settings, heading departments, teams and advising colleagues. These include working in all phases and particularly with disaffected adolescents, their families and teachers. She has travelled widely and came across Circle Time in the United States. She has a particular interest in emotional literacy and is currently researching in this field.

Circles, PSHE and Citizenship

Assessing the Value of Circle Time in Secondary School

Marilyn Tew, Mary Read and Hilary Potter

Paul Chapman
Publishing

Paul Chapman Publishing
A SAGE Publications Company
1 Oliver's Yard
55 City Road
London EC1Y 1SP

SAGE Publications Inc.
2455 Teller Road
Thousand Oaks, California 91320

SAGE Publications India Pvt Ltd
B 1/I 1 Mohan Cooperative Industrial Area
Mathura Road, Post Bag 7 New Delhi 110 044

SAGE Publications Asia-Pacific Pte Ltd
33 Pekin Street #02-01
Far East Square
Singapore 048763

www.luckyduck.co.uk

Commissioning editors: Barbara Maines and George Robinson

Library of Congress Control Number: 2006901497

British Library Cataloguing in Publication data

A catalogue record for this book is available from the British Library

ISBN 978 1 4129 1186 3

Typeset by C&M Digitals (P) Ltd., Chennai, India
Printed on paper from sustainable resources
Printed in Great Britain by The Cromwell Press, Trowbridge, Wiltshire

Contents

Acknowledgements

The achievements of the Faculty of Self, Health and Exercise at Hayesfield School from 1998 to 2003 would not have been possible without the encouragement and support given by the then Head Teacher John Batholomew. Our thanks go to him for facilitating this work. Thank you too to the PSHE teaching team for their professionalism, enthusiasm and good humour. They turned a job into a pleasure over the five years of the project. Finally, we need to acknowledge that Circle Time would not be possible without the willing engagement of the pupils. So our thanks go to them for making Circle Time special and for joining us in reviewing their experiences.

Foreword

The publication of *Circles, PSHE and Citizenship* is a milestone in the history of Circle Time. For many years, Circle Time has been widely used in primary schools yet it is still a relatively unknown learning process at secondary level. This practically oriented book makes a case for the use and benefits of Circle Time in secondary schools, particularly in connection with personal social and health education (PSHE) and Citizenship curricula.

The authors – Marilyn Tew, Mary Read and Hilary Potter – draw on in-depth experiences of implementing Circle Time in several secondary schools and research in one school over five years. Their approach is to set the adoption of Circle Time in the context of challenges in whole-school development in which the PSHE and Citizenship curriculum can be brought alive and become relevant to students' engagement in their personal and social learning, enabling and empowering them to grow, change and develop. The authors unpack the ecology of teaching and learning in circles, making explicit some of the hidden qualities of good pedagogy and the support teachers need in order to extend their practices.

While considering some underlying theoretical concepts of Circle Time, such as self-esteem, locus of control and learning relationships, the text focuses on practical issues and the tips that teachers need to run effective learning in circles. Structure is critical to successful Circle Time, with different phases (beginning, middle and closing) and variations in routine, groupings and use of other strategies within the circle. A major section offers lesson plans for PSHE and Citizenship through Circle Time for 11- to 18-year-olds, dealing with such relevant topics as bullying, body image, sexual issues, rules and risks. The authors describe many games and resources to support participation and exploration in the process of learning in the circle. Skills of listening and speaking, developing an atmosphere of honesty and trust in the group and individual authenticity are essential to the handling of sensitive and controversial issues and the examination of attitudes and values which are at the heart of adolescence.

This guidebook demonstrates how the techniques of Circle Time, rooted in primary education, can be adapted to bridge the gap and provide continuity between primary and secondary schools' approaches to PSHE and Citizenship, where group-based learning and student participation are key. It offers much-needed sources and support for PSHE specialists, Heads of Year and House and all teachers who seek to be inclusive of students in their social and personal education at a time when they are developing their own voices and a greater awareness of learning contexts and relationships. Undertaken well, Circle Time can be an effective, valuable and valued strategy for PSHE and Citizenship learning. This clearly written book offers models based in experience which can be easily adapted by teachers to aid the social and emotional aspects of learning so complementary to the academic curriculum.

Monica J. Taylor
Editor, *Journal of Moral Education*
Research Associate, University of London, Institute of Education

Postscript

I have noticed that there are two main types of educational initiatives. The first come from the 'top', are introduced blanket fashion countrywide, and often cause much stress to the people who have to implement them. They are often changed at vast expense while bringing little benefit to the pupils. The other kind come from the other end of the spectrum. They often start in one place, where they are welcomed by the people who wish to initiate them, have minimal cost implications and bring huge rewards to the pupils. As you may well guess, Circle Time was one of the latter initiatives in the UK, which may account for its current popularity among teachers and why it takes place in so many classrooms around the land.

As far as I'm aware, Circle Time began when I realised that the well-planned academic curriculum, even when offered by enthusiastic and competent teachers, was not enough to cater for the true needs of the children. If they were going to feel emotionally stable enough to want to learn and behave well, a new approach was necessary. So the children sat on the floor in a circle and I sat with them as the first Circle Time took place. The strategy that I used came from my experiential studies in humanistic psychology and knowledge of similar work being done in other countries. From virtually the first moment, the first laugh, the first look of understanding, the first one of concentration, the first smile of one child to another, it became obvious that something of great value was taking place. Daily Circle Times followed in all the classes in the school and the statements of staff who began to see the changes in their charges confirmed that the time involved in this practice was being invested well. Over time, educational advisers showed interest and others came to join in the circles and workshops and so awareness of Circle Time increased throughout Cambridgeshire and then beyond.

When, in 1989, my article 'Magic Circles' was published in the *TES* there was a massive positive response from readers from abroad as well as the UK and an acknowledgement of the value of the participation of pupils in Circle Times was well established. The tremendous potential they had for good in the lives of children was clearly recognised by many teachers who adopted the idea and began to conduct their own circles. Now, nearly 20 years later, Circle Time gets official recommendations in government literature.

This book is a first-class contribution to the ever-expanding literature on Circle Time and I welcome it for two reasons.

In the first instance, self-esteem is a much-maligned term and advocates who promote its importance for young people constantly face criticism from many people who use myths and misunderstandings to make their case. It is easy to find research in support of self-esteem, however. The conclusion of the 1970 *British Cohort Study*, published in July 2003, states that children with plenty of self-esteem enjoyed better chances of success as adults. Dr Neil Smelser, co-editor of The *Social Importance of Self-Esteem*, reviewed over 30,000 studies and concluded that low self-esteem was the root cause of many social problems. He believed, as I do, that self-esteem is central to ameliorating many of the problems we see in schools today. If you are a teacher and can invest in the time to obtain the skills to facilitate great Circle Times, you will have the tremendous satisfaction of seeing so many of the positive qualities you wish for your pupils emerge and flourish.

Secondly, for a long time Circle Time was thought of only as a primary school activity. Now the authors of this volume, and others, recognise that secondary school pupils should not be denied the advantages that taking part in this process can give them. Mary Read, with wise advice and help from consultants Marilyn Tew and Hilary Potter, have successfully incorporated it into their school organisation in Bath and written this as a guide for others to do the same. I hope many will read it and be inspired to do so. It is well structured and easy to find your way about. For newcomers it has a clear exposition of what you need to take into account so that you and your pupils will gain much from the experience. If you already conduct Circle Time, it has lots of good ideas and suggestions for you to use.

Circle Times have a lot going for them. Whether you have low self-esteem or high self-esteem there is always something to be gained by taking part. In circles I have run, I've witnessed good things happen for the youngest child and the oldest grownup. I would recommend Circle Times for parents and their families, for learners of every age as they progress through the education system, and for all adults as they go through life.

There should be a television advertisement telling everyone how good they are!

Murray White
UK Representative, International Council for Self-Esteem

Introduction

This book is about bringing personal, social and health education alive and making it relevant to the lives of the young people who receive it. In other words, it is about transforming personal, social and health education (PSHE) and Citizenship into personal and social development (PSD). The main theme of the book is about using a circle and a process called Circle Time as the vehicle for engaging learners in secondary school in their own personal and social learning so that they grow, change and develop as a result. It is a conscious attempt to make the learning processes such as being able to take part, to accommodate other people's views, to listen and to speak appropriately, equally important to a young person's personal and social development as the factual content of the PSHE or Citizenship lesson.

The contents of the book are based on a five-year piece of in-depth practical research based in a secondary school in the city of Bath. The learning is not confined to one school, however, and has been applied in many other secondary schools across the UK. These schools are committed to making PSHE and Citizenship curricula relevant and life-changing by planning lessons and experiences that stimulate personal and social development in their students.

How to use this book

The book is divided into five main sections. The first section presents the case for Circle Time in secondary schools and considers some of the reasons why this approach has not been widely adopted. This section also includes some insights from Hayesfield school in Bath as a case study for managers and leaders who might want to look at using Circle Time in their own schools.

Section Two gives the theoretical and practical information that teachers need in order to be able to run effective circles. We have tried to present the theory in a user-friendly way so that busy teachers can dip into different sections and topics without having to read everything. Section Three looks in detail at Circle Time as an approach to PSHE and Citizenship topics. It presents the practical issues that need to be addressed in order to run successful circle lessons. This section also answers some of the questions that teachers ask most frequently and gives some pointers for further reading and training for those who want to take the ideas and develop them.

Section Four presents a selection of lesson plans that can be used for running Circle Time lessons across the entire school age range from 11- to 18-year-olds. All the lesson plans have been tried with students at the age and stage indicated. They last between 50 minutes and an hour, depending on the timetable constraints of the school. Some lessons also have suggested homework or extension activities which teachers can use as written, or adapt to meet their own needs. The lesson plans are called circle scripts. They can be used as a basis for planning and writing customised scripts to meet the needs of your particular students.

Finally, the fifth section gives a selection of games and resources for use in Circle Time lessons at secondary school. All the games have been used in a secondary context with boys and girls and with all ages. Different games have different appeal to different groups, however, and we suggest that you try a variety of games with your groups until you find the kind of game they like the best. It then becomes possible to use the group to develop the game and come up with your own variations.

Useful resources for running circles

Many of the suggested resources are specific to particular lessons and the ones that relate to scripts in Section Four are presented in the fifth section of the book. Some resources are useful for all Circle Time lessons, however. If teachers have these resources on hand, they have the flexibility to use them if the need arises, or can leave them to one side if the circle runs well without them. Resources that should be available in any Circle Time lesson include:

- ▶ large sheets of paper to capture group thinking
- ▶ coloured pens
- ▶ an optional speaking object that the group can pass round the circle to ensure that everyone gets an opportunity to express their view (a speaking object is very useful for younger students and becomes less useful as the students increase in age, or become more skilled at working in a circle)
- ▶ a class set of pens so that students don't have to carry their own
- ▶ small strips of paper for student views
- ▶ a box or hat for collecting anonymous written views.

The CD-ROM contains PDF files, labelled Examples of Circle Scripts and Resources and Games for Circle Time which consists of work-sheets for each lesson in this resource. You will need Acrobat Reader version 3 or higher to view and print these resources.

The documents are set up to print to A4 but you can enlarge them to A3 by increasing the output percentage at the point of printing using the page setup settings for your printer.

To photocopy the worksheets directly from this book, set your photocopier to enlarge by 125% and align the edge of the page to be copied against the leading edge of the copier glass (usually indicated by an arrow).

Section One

The case for Circle Time

Ever since personal and social education became recognised as an important part of a school's educational purpose, researchers, trainers and practitioners have agreed that active, participatory groupwork is a key element in engaging young people in their own personal and social development. More recently, in 1999, Citizenship was added to the National Curriculum as a foundation subject. At the heart of the Citizenship programme of study lies skills for developing inquiry, communication, participation and responsible action. Here, as in PSHE, is a focus on dynamic groupwork, which requires students to meet face to face so that they have to interact directly with one another.

In conventional classrooms, students put up their hands to show that they have an answer to a question, or a view on an issue and the teacher chooses who will speak. Quieter or less confident students rarely volunteer their view in these lessons and unwanted views can be 'screened out' by a teacher according to which students they choose and do not choose.

> "I never get to say my view because the teacher knows that I don't agree with her." (Girl aged 15)

When groupwork is used, however, tasks are presented so that students work in pairs, small groups or as a whole-class group. In these lessons, the ability to work with other people is as much a learning outcome as completing the activity itself. Students are expected to use skills such as co-operation, listening, communication and accommodation so that they can work together to complete the activities. However, any one of us who has done much groupwork will know that this is not always straightforward. It is likely that we can all recall times when groupwork has been successful and other times when it has been a dismal failure. Sometimes the more able or vocal students 'take over'. They may organise the others, produce the ideas and distribute the resources. The quieter or more reflective students are often not heard and many a good idea is consequently lost. Unless students are taught how to work in a group, they do not develop the relevant skills. At best they work independently, only bringing the work together to present it at the end. At worst they become overtly angry or make it impossible for the rest of the group to complete the task. Time needs to be given to learning the skills of groupwork. Sadly, the development of an effective group does not happen just because the people are put together (as any of us who have been on committees know only too well!).

Group processes certainly begin when a mix of people are put in a room together, but being able to work co-operatively with other people requires the acquisition of a set of skills and a journey in self-awareness. Only as a teacher intervenes to promote group development does the collection of individual students begin to form the esffective functioning unit that is called a group. Group development follows a set of stages and at each stage, students must learn to cope with new problems and develop new skills and attitudes. As the group develops, so the group members:

▶ find more productive ways of working together
▶ develop trust in one another
▶ become open to new experience
▶ improve their communication
▶ feel freer to participate actively in classroom activities and learning.

In order to promote effective group functioning, some secondary schools are building on the work started by their partner primary schools, and are using Circle Time as the main approach to teaching and learning in PSHE and Citizenship lessons.

The power of a circle

Circle Time is a group process that involves the whole class sitting on chairs in a circle so that every member of the group can see and be seen by every other group member. It has the advantage that no member of the group can hide; each one has to take his place as part of the group in order for the class to become a productive and fully functioning unit that can consider issues, solve problems, reach conclusions and plan for action. The geometric configuration of the circle makes it possible for each member of the group to interact with any other. The teacher ceases to be the only focal point of discussion and students look at one another, responding directly to contributions and suggestions made by their peers. As the class group members become more skilled at speaking, listening, waiting for their turn, considering the impact of their words and finding more helpful ways of voicing their opinion, so the quality of the dialogue improves and the teacher takes a less prominent role. It is possible to eventually arrive at a place where a class member leads the circle and the teacher becomes part of the group.

Circles have been used when schools want to improve the quality of interaction and engagement in PSHE and Citizenship lessons. This has often been because students find it harder to acquire factual information about curriculum topics, without being challenged or having to consider how the issues under discussion impact on personal choices and decision making. Circle Time also provides continuity for students as they move from primary to secondary school. Many primary schools use Circle Time and the students have regular opportunities to discuss issues in the circle for at least some part of their primary schooling. For some children Circle Time has been a weekly feature of school life throughout primary school. Indeed, Circle Time is recommended by the Department for Education and Skills (DfES) in the SEAL (Social and Emotional Aspects of Learning) programme as an ideal vehicle for active student participation and school improvement. When these students come to secondary school, they look for the same opportunities to speak, to be heard, to discuss and to problem solve.

The benefits of Circle Time

The experience of secondary schools that have adopted Circle Time for PSHE and Citizenship lessons is that it is surprisingly successful. Teachers who were unsure about adopting a new approach with more challenging classes have been pleasantly surprised at the positive response of the students and the beneficial impact of working in a circle.

> "I think Circle Time is excellent as a way of delivering PSE. I would not like to teach PSE [now] in any other way – the discussions seem more involved and it is more difficult for dominant members of the tutor group to 'hijack' a discussion. I find it easier to create new groups and split up cliques". (PSHE teacher)
>
> "Prior to Circle Time training, I would have described myself as a teacher who was 'uncomfortable' with open forum discussions and role play. The Circle Time way of delivering PSE has altered my views and as a former sceptic I am now very positive about this teaching method." (History teacher)

As we have listened to the students in response to Circle Time lessons, we have discovered that it can help the individual student grow and develop in self-awareness and awareness of other people. Students develop more positive behaviour because they are provided with a place to recognise that their emotions and reactions are affected by others and that other people's emotions and reactions affect them. Students improve the quality of their speaking and listening. The confidence of quieter members of the group increases and better relationships are established student to student and between teacher and students. *'In a circle you can say what you actually feel'* (Student aged 13). The circle becomes a place of acceptance and support in secondary school life and over time, a supportive group develops from a disparate class of students. *'It's like getting closer when we are sat in a circle'* (Student aged 12).

Once the group is supportive, this becomes a place to examine attitudes, values and issues relating to personal, social and health education. *'At the beginning we didn't say what we actually thought but now we do'* (Student aged 13). Students are encouraged to take responsibility for their views, opinions, responses and actions. *'It doesn't matter what your opinion is. It is your opinion'* (Student aged 13). In other words the circle contributes to a more internal locus of control. These lessons make a significant contribution to developing and sustaining a high level of self-esteem in students.

Reasons for introducing Circle Time

Whenever we go into other schools to talk about using Circle Time for PSHE and Citizenship, we get asked to identify what it is that motivates a secondary school to take on this approach to teaching and learning. This is not an easy task as every school is unique. We have, however, tried to pull together information from schools that have successfully implemented circles as an established way of working. We are not saying that each factor is equally important or that all have to be present if Circle Time is to succeed. Rather they are pointers to the sort of issues and conditions that might act as levers for change. The first impetus for introducing Circle Time quite often comes from senior management. They may recognise an imbalance between the academic and pastoral life of the school with a weighting on the side of achievement and standards. The imbalance might well have resulted in a cut in PSHE teaching time. Reduced time makes it even more imperative to ensure that teaching and learning are as effective as possible in this area of the curriculum. Senior management may also recognise that school structures make it difficult for tutors to maintain a consistent relationship with their groups. Split-site schools present particular challenges when tutors are not always available to register their own groups. Sometimes, the pressure for change comes from the students themselves, when a survey or questionnaire reveals inequality of experience in PSHE. Some teachers or tutors are outstanding and some quietly choose to avoid the curriculum, so some students do not receive a positive experience in their PSHE entitlement. Similarly, students in their first year of secondary school can arrive with experience of circles in primary school and an expectation that they will have similar opportunities to talk and share their views.

The pressure for change might also come from teaching staff with a request for training in groupwork skills and different classroom management techniques. Someone might have been on an external course and come back to the school enthused with a need to change. The introduction of Circle Time needs a core number of people who have a vision to introduce and implement this kind of groupwork. It can start with a single enthusiast such as a Head of Year who is able to persuade a tutor team to 'give it a go'. Or the pressure from teaching staff may arise from an increase in more challenging student behaviour which causes teachers to look for tools and techniques to support holding classroom dialogue and discussion of any quality.

On the other hand, the pressure for change might come from outside the school, from government initiatives that require schools to develop in this area. Recent initiatives have placed particular emphasis on student participation and hearing student voices (Every Child Matters and the new Office for Standards in Education (Ofsted) inspection framework). Another relevant initiative is the recent work on social and emotional aspects of learning (SEAL) in primary schools, which is being extended and developed for secondary schools. External pressure can also take the form of financial support for training which can come in various forms such as the 'inclusion budget' or PSHE accreditation.

Blocks and constraints to change

The introduction of any new initiative in schools inevitably has to overcome a number of obstacles, particularly in an era of initiative overload and teacher exhaustion. One of the most significant blocks to investing time and money in introducing Circle Time has been the perception that it is a luxury compared to other pressing needs in the school. Schools have had to address some or all of the blocks and constraints listed below in order to get the support and resources needed to introduce Circle Time as a way of working in PSHE and Citizenship.

We have listed the blocks and constraints so that you can decide which, if any, apply in your situation. You will then be better placed to work out a plan for collecting the evidence, or to put together a proposal that will give you the best chance of obtaining the resources you will need. The major constraints we have found are:

▶   There is always a range of different subject areas, faculties and school initiatives looking for developmental time and money.
▶   There may be specialist school targets to be met such as Technology College, Expressive and Performing Arts, Sports, Languages, and Circle Time is not seen to readily fit in.

- ▶ There may be serious questions about whether we should be investing training in behaviour management when the standards agenda is more pressing.
- ▶ This area of the curriculum often has a dearth of hard data to support the idea of Circle Time. The Circle Time initiative runs the risk of appearing somewhat like an 'act of faith'. You could be asked to provide a risk assessment on its implementation.

Needless to say it is unlikely that everyone will be in favour, no matter what kind of initiative you want to introduce. If Circle Time is to succeed in your school, it needs to have a cogent argument in its favour, preferably supported by some hard evidence (Taylor, 2003). It is best presented from faculty level with recognition and support from someone at senior leadership level.

Current levers for change in education

- ▶ PSHE and Citizenship curricula (National Curriculum Framework 2000)
- ▶ Every Child Matters (Children Act 2004)
- ▶ Spiritual, Moral, Social and Cultural (SMSC) development in the new Ofsted inspection framework
- ▶ Hearing pupil voices
- ▶ SEAL (Social and Emotional Aspects of Learning)
- ▶ Healthy Schools (particularly emotional health and wellbeing)
- ▶ Anti-bullying policy and practice
- ▶ Investors In People accreditation
- ▶ Chartermark.

Case study of Circle Time – Hayesfield school, Bath

Hayesfield comprehensive school in Bath introduced Circle Time as part of a whole-school approach to PSHE and Citizenship. The pressure of increasing demands for higher academic grades had squeezed the time for PSHE in the school. At the same time, Citizenship was introduced as a new foundation subject in the National Curriculum. The result was a conflict of interests that created a real sense of urgency among staff to find ways of making the allotted curriculum time count. They wanted to stimulate meaningful debate about issues and engage the students in examining their values and attitudes. It seemed important to involve them in decision making that might impact on their lives inside and outside school, rather than merely covering the curriculum content and presenting factual information. Challenging and changing values and attitudes are difficult tasks for any of us. If the school was to help the students to look at their thinking, feelings and behaviour in a meaningful way, teaching and learning methods that both permitted and promoted open and honest discussion were of paramount importance. In the quest for more appropriate ways of delivering the PSHE curriculum, the school began to explore the role of groups, group dynamics and classroom interactions, both student–student and teacher–student, that might support the personal and social development of its students.

As the debate about effective PSHE took place at Hayesfield, a similar debate was taking place at the national level. Between 1996 and 2005, a large number of publications was produced by the Qualifications and Curriculum Authority (QCA), the DfES and Ofsted to support schools in their implementation of aspects of values development in schools, spiritual, moral, social and cultural development, personal, social and health education and Citizenship. A recurrent theme in all these documents, including the National Curriculum schemes of work for Citizenship was a focus on teaching approaches. In particular, they advocated experiential learning and active participation in groups. "Teaching should ensure that knowledge and understanding about becoming informed citizens are acquired and applied when developing skills of enquiry and communication and participation and responsible action" (QCA, 1999, p. 184). Senior leadership teams in schools constantly face the dilemma of how to keep the staff sane while facing and implementing multiple new initiatives. They have to deliver statutory requirements, but they need to bear in mind 'What matters?', 'What is important for our school?', 'What will make a difference?'

Alongside all other senior management teams, those at Hayesfield considered the way forward for their school in relation to these new initiatives. One of the important factors for them was engaging the values and opinions of young people. The effective use of groupwork emerged as a key to the kind of lessons they wanted to see. Teachers who are familiar with the principles that underpin the forming and functioning of a group are able to confidently plan and facilitate such lessons. Teaching in PSHE and Citizenship called for the skills of reflection, enquiry, communication and active participation. Lessons that develop these skills require teachers who are:

▶ able to give attention to the way the group is working as well as noticing how individual students are managing the learning tasks
▶ adept at enabling a group to function effectively and know when to intervene and when to leave the group to sort itself out without adult involvement
▶ familiar with the processes and principles of group dynamics and have practised the skills of groupwork
▶ willing to make the emotional and intellectual investments needed to understand group processes because they have discovered that when a group of individuals can function as a unit, learning increases, behavioural problems decrease and personal and social development takes place for all members of the group.

Introducing a new way of working is never that easy, however. The decision was taken to introduce Circle Time at Key Stage 3. Once it was established in the first three years, for students aged 11–14, a review was planned to look at how to extend its use into the fourth and fifth years and then into the sixth form. In order to get even the first phase of the plan underway the school had to overcome a number of obstacles: convincing enough people on the Senior Management Team (SMT); finding the money; and finding the right time to undertake the training. Once the initial phase of implementation was over, the next obstacles were how to maintain the training and funding over a period of several years so that Circle Time could become properly embedded. A further practical issue was how to find enough rooms where the furniture could be rearranged into a circle to accommodate a class of 30. Once this was addressed, there were the issues of how to overcome complaints from some staff in adjoining classes about the noise of furniture being moved and games being played and how to accommodate the staff who actively found ways to be timetabled away from the Lower School site so that they could avoid taking part in Circle Time in their role as a tutor!

If you have been teaching for a length of time, you will appreciate that trends in education tend to be circular. The debate as to who would be best placed to deliver PSHE and active Citizenship is one such circular debate. The content a student needs in PSHE is constantly changing, as are the staff who teach it. Consequently, schools need to regularly monitor and review its impact and success. Circle Time was introduced into PSHE in the first year, taught by form tutors. An evaluation at the end of the year made it clear that, while Circle Time was mostly successful when facilitated by tutors, a move to specialist PSHE teams would be even better.

In a staff survey it was apparent that many tutors did not have the confidence or interest to deliver the PSHE or Citizenship curriculum well. As a result, some creative thinking took place and gave birth to a new faculty that encompassed Citizenship, PSHE and physical education (PE), with a brief to extend extra-curricular activities and to raise the profile of healthy living for all students and even staff. The new faculty was called SHE (Self, Health and Exercise) and it enabled students to have a holistic experience of healthy living, from theory to practice; an important message for life. The new faculty became the specialist team which used Circle Time work to deliver this part of the curriculum.

When the new faculty was launched it aimed to:

▶ Teach PSHE and Citizenship every week.
▶ Teach PSHE using staff who wanted to teach it. This resulted in all Heads of Year, Assistant Heads of Year, the PE Department and enthusiasts who wanted to be part of the team becoming members of the new SHE faculty. The majority of them had already had circle training as part of the ongoing programme.
▶ Rewrite the whole of the PSHE and Citizenship curriculum, a task shared among the team, and to deliver as much of the curriculum as possible through circles from the first to the fifth years (ages 11–16).

The way ahead for Hayesfield

Often in schools good ideas come and go. How often have you experienced inspirational training for it to be lost within weeks?

Challenges lay ahead to keep the philosophy of circles at the heart of the curriculum designed to promote students' personal and social development. An evaluation at the end of the first year of implementation showed that a team of 15 staff had been trained in the use of circles. All had prepared and shared PSHE and Citizenship lessons based on a Circle Time format. They had delivered the curriculum from the first to the fifth years, with some staff teaching in every year group. Their commitment and professionalism was, and still is, phenomenal. Yet to embed Circle Time in the ethos of PSHE at Hayesfield school, we would have to:

▶ maintain the quality of delivery and enthusiasm of staff and students
▶ become independent in training ourselves so that we could keep our skill levels high and introduce new staff to this way of working
▶ refresh ideas and encourage staff who felt less successful
▶ continue to write circle lessons for each other and be open to feedback about successes and failures
▶ review the lesson pro-forma for circles
▶ ensure that Circle Time lessons kept student participation as a priority
▶ modify Circle Time for older students
▶ become more confident in designing circles to meet our school's needs as they arose
▶ extend the training to include other agencies working with our students in school
▶ continue to monitor and evaluate the work including observing colleagues as they ran circles and inviting other people in so that we maintained consistent quality across the team
▶ acknowledge and appreciate the efforts and achievements of the teaching team and students involved.

"It has been a delight to watch the staff become confident to use Circle Time in PSHE and other lessons. The relationships with students have visibly improved and both staff and students enjoy the lessons much more." (Deputy Head Teacher)

Section Two

The theory behind Circle Time

Introducing any new way of working requires training and Circle Time is no exception. In the Hayesfield case study, training in Circle Time strategies and activities took place over an extended period of time and included both practical and theoretical elements. The training was modified and extended in response to staff needs as Circle Time was implemented and until it became established as part of the school's teaching and learning practice. The Hayesfield experience is typical of schools that have taken on this way of working and we thought it would be helpful to readers if we presented an indication of the sort of training schools need when introducing this kind of work.

Training can take place in July, after the end of GCSE and A level exams or early in September. The advantages of summer term training are that training events require less cover because exam classes have been lost. In addition, staff are trained and ready for the beginning of the new year and they have time to practise using a circle in the last few weeks of term and to use that experience in September. The down-side of summer term training is that it is unlikely that all new members of staff will be released from their current posts to attend the training event, leaving a number of staff untrained at the beginning of September. Some schools, however, do manage to bring in new staff for the day or half-day of training.

Putting the training at the beginning of a new academic year overcomes the problem of an incomplete team. Any new members of staff that have just joined the school will be available for September training, though they may be so overloaded with trying to cope in the new situation that they can't absorb a new approach to PSHE and Citizenship on top of everything else. The disadvantage of overload might be overcome by having two training experiences organised in the same term, with time for staff to try out the ideas between the two sessions and review their learning in the second. There is no ideal training model and schools have to make their decisions based on the best possible solution at the time.

It is often helpful to use an outside trainer, however, as a fresh voice and professional training add significance to the initiative. Evaluations of staff and students' experiences are important in deciding what training to provide next. Often a team of staff will look for 'refreshing' and new ideas rather than formal training. Yet there is always a small number of staff new to the school or team who will need training from the beginning. Whenever new members of the teaching team are not trained, the momentum of Circle Time will be lost and it will take that much longer to embed the practice.

Sometimes, a Local Education Authority (LEA) will support training in circles for teachers completing the Certificate in Professional Development in PSHE. This allows staff from several schools to update their skills. A notable feature of this kind of training is that it is often multi-agency. It can be difficult for a school to retain a consistent ethos of delivery in PSHE when working with outside agencies. If professionals linked to the school such as health workers and police can be trained at the same time as the teaching staff, it becomes much easier to maintain consistency of approach for the students.

The amount of time available for training will depend on the funding stream and the level of commitment to Circle Time. Some schools may want to train a relatively small group of teachers such as tutors in a year team or a specialist PSHE and Citizenship teaching team. In other schools, the commitment might be much greater and extend to a whole key stage, whole staff, or across different aspects of the curriculum.

Similarly, some schools may want to stage the training across several consecutive years while others may want to train all the staff in a particular key stage at one time, or even to provide whole-staff training on one or two training days. The choice of training model will depend on the bigger vision held by the senior management of the school, the budget, other demands for available training time and the degree of change that is needed to implement this way of working in the school.

Whatever the model of training, there are some topics and skills that are crucial to a teacher's ability to run an effective Circle Time. Perhaps unusually in the realm of continuing professional development, learning to run Circle Time calls for much more than knowledge and understanding. Teachers also have to acquire, practise and hone their skills of facilitation and inter-personal communication which are different from those used in other teaching and learning contexts.

Overview of theoretical topics

The topics covered in training sessions include:

- self-esteem
- locus of control
- stages of group life
- groundrules
- learning relationships
- teacher as role-model
- listening and dialogue
- controversial and sensitive issues
- professional learning buddies.

Self-esteem

"The importance of perceiving oneself in positive ways can hardly be overstressed for when one holds such a concept of oneself, one tends to expect success. By thinking in this way, one is likely to bring about this fortunate outcome through the mechanism of the self-fulfilling prophecy. Success seems to breed success, and failure seems to breed failure." (Burns, 1982, p. 365)

Teachers who want to use Circle Time need a good understanding of the factors that influence a person's self-esteem and the behaviours that relate to high and to low self-evaluation. Poor behaviour in school is often perceived to be anti-establishment or deliberately designed by the student to disrupt. Yet studies in self-esteem demonstrate that low self-esteem can result in self-protective behaviours which can look like aggression, antagonism, disruption or passivity. Low self-esteem is counter-productive to doing well in school. It causes young people to disengage from the learning environment, to avoid risk and protect what little esteem they have. These strategies often result in students' rejection of positive overtures from supportive and helpful adults, while continuing to behave in a way that is consistent with the poor view they have of themselves. The good news is that a person's perception of herself and consequently her evaluation of herself (self-esteem) can change. Specific, affirming feedback, which counteracts the student's poor self-image and is offered in an accepting and non-judgemental way, can improve self-esteem (Brophy, 1981). Research into Circle Time indicates that circle work can provide the context for receiving feedback that provides a more positive image of self (Canfield, 1990; Taylor, 2003; White, 1991; 1998).

"There are some students that get seen in a positive light during Circle Time. There's one person, not necessarily the best in the class, but they can see themselves knowing more than others and being confident. Some of the academically weaker children can know more and can say 'I know about this, it's called this, and this can happen.' They have often experienced more things and have something to talk about. Often if they are academically weak, they are at the bottom all the time. They come to Circle Time and there is a level playing field." (PSHE teacher)

Implications for practice

Regular, positive and affirming experiences in the peer group have an impact on students' self-concept and their respect for themselves and other people. The key seems to lie in the teacher's ability to set and maintain a safe and inclusive emotional climate. Trust, respect and mutually supportive relationships can only develop in emotional safety. Climate setting is partly about establishing and sustaining good groundrules, such as noticing the put-downs when they occur, including the subtle or hidden ones and challenging them by making them the subject of discussion. It is also about the teacher being the relational role model. Students watch adults very carefully and they pick up and mirror the teacher's mood, attitudes and even prejudices. It is important that teachers are fair, inclusive and affirming to all students in the group so that every student receives helpful feedback that supports a positive self-image.

"The tutors have the biggest impact on the circle. They don't have their favourites but treat us all equally." (Student aged 13)
"Self-esteem definitely increases as they feel valued and they are not laughed at or commented on. They all have their 15 seconds of fame!" (Taylor, 2003, p. 39)

Practical tips

1. Take a few minutes to be calm and positive before you begin the circle lesson.
2. Regularly examine your preferences and prejudices in relation to students.
3. Ensure that every student has regular opportunities to receive good news about themselves and/or their work.
4. Play games and organise activities in the circle that give students the opportunity to lead or 'be someone' even if only for a moment.
5. Ensure that you are looking after your own self-esteem so that you have enough emotional energy to give to the students.

Locus of control

"A locus of control orientation is a belief about whether the outcomes of our actions are contingent on what we do (internal control orientation) or on events outside our personal control (external control orientation." Zimbardo, 1969, p. 275)

The theory that underpins locus of control suggests that people differ in the measure to which they believe that events they experience are caused by or are a consequence of their actions. Adults and children with an internal locus of control are inclined to take responsibility for their actions. They are not easily influenced by the opinions of others and tend to do better at tasks when they can work at their own pace. By comparison, people with an external locus of control tend to blame outside circumstances for their mistakes and credit their successes to luck rather than to their own efforts.

Young people, especially those who are disaffected and disturbed, tend to have an external locus of control. This means they believe that events are not a result of their effort or behaviour but are influenced by chance, luck, or some other outside factor beyond their control or power to change. These are the ones who are likely to say 'It wasn't my fault, she made me', or 'I just wasn't very lucky with the questions in the test'. They don't feel able to take responsibility for their own actions, and don't believe they can bring about improvement in their behaviour or school work. Those who have an internal locus of control, on the other hand, believe that there is a strong causal relationship between their behaviour and subsequent events. They therefore continually strive to achieve the effects they want. People who have an internal locus of control have a highly developed sense of efficacy, that is, they feel confident that they can find a solution to a problem, even if the problem is hard to solve.

> "A strong sense of intellectual efficacy fosters a high level of motivation, academic accomplishments and development of intrinsic interest in academic subject matter." (Bandura, 1997, p. 174)

Many of the activities of Circle Time are planned to influence locus of control. Students are encouraged to think about actions, events and consequences in the safety of the circle. One of the recurrent themes in Circle Time is problem solving, which may involve hypothetical scenarios, or real-life events that the class group face. Choice-making and problem-solving techniques can then be transferred to other contexts, moving the locus of control from external to internal.

> "There is a big push on assessment for learning and the circle is a really good way of doing it. The students all want to say something and very rarely choose to pass. They discuss the things they've understood and not understood and feel better when they find it's not just them that didn't understand. We make up class rules about what motivates them in the

subject and they can decide how I'm going to treat them in the year and suddenly a big bond of trust appears between the teacher and the class. Sometimes students who understood a topic explain it to the rest of the group in a better way than I can and so everyone learns." (Maths teacher)

Implications for practice

Developing and encouraging students' internal locus of control is not a 'quick fix' process. It takes time and persistence. Circle Time activities that encourage looking at a range of situations and considering a breadth of possible outcomes are helpful. These can be set up as 'Agony Aunt', role-play exercises, hypothetical scenarios or issues that are anonymously suggested by the group. When students are encouraged to view situations from different perspectives and make choices about how characters might respond, alongside thinking about how they would personally respond in a situation, they begin to see the connection between choices, actions and outcomes. In the example, the teacher uses a circle session as part of his assessment. He gets feedback on students' understanding, gives advice on ways to achieve better success and the group provides their peers with strategies for improving performance. Students see the connection between effort, motivation, choice and success.

Practical tips

1. Provide some opportunities for problem solving.
2. Use scenarios that invite an empathic response so students can identify with the characters and issues.
3. Challenge the notion that life is a series of serendipitous events over which we have no control and set up situations where people could and did influence the outcomes by their effort and choice making.
4. Give the group opportunities to influence situations in their school life.
5. Provide opportunities for review and feedback about good outcomes so that the connection is made between effort, choice and outcome.

Stages of group life

Running Circle Time sessions requires an understanding of the development of a group through time. It can be helpful to think of each Circle Time session as a small, short-lived replica of the entire life of a group. Tuckman (1973) identified five stages in the development of an effective group:

▶ *Forming* – the stage when the group is first established
▶ *Norming* – establishing ways of working together
▶ *Storming* – finding ways of productively dealing with conflict in the group
▶ *Performing* – becoming a productive working unit
▶ *Mourning* – ending the group.

It is useful to think about the life of a group in terms of the model of group development and to ensure that attention is given to each of the stages. This is particularly relevant when students either join or leave the group as the dynamics will automatically change. Whenever the composition of a group changes, members need to re-establish their position.

> "The 15-year-olds had spent their first three years of secondary school getting comfortable with a tutor group. They were all jumbled up at the beginning of their fourth year into new tutor groups and were in with people they had perhaps only ever seen in the corridor. It has taken about nine months of Circle Time to develop a good level of security and safety and I feel they are more cohesive now, able to work outside their immediate friendship groups." (PSHE teacher)

Implications for practice

Perhaps one of the most difficult things to remember in a school context with a large curriculum to cover and limited contact time is how long it takes to establish a group. The students can take many weeks to feel comfortable with one another. Yet there will be no quality of honest or open interaction without a high level of trust and comfort in the group. Similarly, there can be an assumption that by the fourth year of secondary school, students should know how to behave in a classroom setting. No time is therefore given to establishing group norms for the way this group will 'be' together.

Time and time again, teachers and students say that it took a long time for the group to gel, for the trust to be established and discussion to become productive. Experience suggests that if time and attention are given to the group processes early on in the life of the group, then norms are established early and there is a greater chance of productive work taking place. Remember though, that the closing of a group at the end of year, a key stage or on leaving this phase of schooling can be very traumatic for group members. Teachers would be well advised to think about rites of passage, rituals for closure and time to look back and forward with the group in order to reduce the unhelpful reactions some students have to losing the familiar and safe environment of their tutor group.

"Every year our tutor has a party that starts us off and finishes the term off well." (Student aged 14)

Practical tips

1. Provide many opportunities for group forming including name games, getting to know you activities and interactive experiences.
2. Ensure that *this* group of students establishes their unique ways of working together by discussing routines and procedures.
3. When conflict arises, see if you can let the group find its own solutions rather than quelling the first signs of unrest by using your teacher authority.
4. Make sure that you take time to allow the group to close properly by reflecting back on their shared history and by looking forward to the next phase of their lives.
5. Be kind to yourself when the group does not function too well. Think about the stage of group life your group has reached and see if you can come up with a way to address the difficulty.

Groundrules

It is helpful to make explicit to students what PSHE and Citizenship are about and to give them the opportunity to establish groundrules for behaviour that would apply to work in the circle and in smaller groups. A class will find it difficult to make groundrules unless they understand the kind of groups they will be expected to work in. For instance, they will sometimes work in a whole circle, sometimes in pairs, in friendship groups and at other times with people who are not friends. They may have to work in groups of even numbers, odd numbers, random groups, gender groups or interest groups. They will always be expected to ensure that nobody is excluded. Once the expectation is set, students can begin to think about what they will see and hear when a group is working well together.

Students who have followed the SEAL programme in primary school will be very familiar with this way of working. From the list of behaviours, they can begin to make groundrules for the ways in which they will work together so that everyone feels comfortable. Groundrules often include: ensuring only one person talks at a time; everyone is involved; no put-downs; listening; making sure everyone gets a chance to speak; everyone has a right to their privacy; and no one *has* to speak. The groundrules form the basis of the way the group will be together. They are an expression of 'the way of doing things round here'.

Another important point here is to ensure that all adults in the circle model the groundrules. There is nothing worse than listening to a student reveal something sensitive and having the moment ruined by an adult raising her eyes to heaven or folding her arms with a sigh!

The groundrules apply to everyone without exception. It is good practice to remind everyone of the agreed groundrules at the start of each lesson to ensure that everyone understands that these rules are not negotiable. However, students with special needs or behaviour problems may need additional support or individual behaviour contracts that they work with. Students need to feel safe and that they will never be forced to speak out or even to move if they feel embarrassed or shy. The atmosphere needs to be warm and accepting but with a steely edge of very assertively applied groundrules that come in if anyone attempts to sabotage the lesson.

"It is difficult to maintain the groundrules without breaking the flow of the circle. If the person speaking is not very confident, then I am most likely to catch the eye of the disrupting person and stop them that way." (PSHE teacher)

"It's not just that people don't keep the rules. It's that they don't care. Teachers don't enforce them. If the teacher lives them, then it works". (Student aged 16)

Implications for practice

Groundrules can be very effective, or entirely inconsequential, according to whether they are seen as a formality or become a lived reality to the group. The examples suggest that by the age of 16 the students are very astute about whether or not teachers believe in and abide by the groundrules. Their verdict was that though groundrules are important, they are often not enforced and therefore they lack impact on the behaviour of the group. In younger years, the situation was very different as one student revealed: *'We set up groundrules at the beginning of the year about keeping issues within the circle and people keep to them. We made groundrules by sitting in a circle and talking about them. They are written in the back of our PSHE books and they are constantly referred to'* (Student aged 12). The initial expectation is that the teacher will remind the group of the groundrules, keep them himself and enforce them. As the group matures, it is desirable to get the group to enforce the groundrules and to hold other group members accountable to them. The more weight the teacher gives to the groundrules, the more likely it is that the students will take them seriously. The groundrules need to be a living, dynamic, visual part of the group, not some agreed and archived information that has no relevance to the group a week or two later. The more visible they are and the more they are referred to, the more likely they are to be respected and adhered to.

Practical tips

1. Involve the whole class in establishing groundrules at the beginning of the year.
2. Make sure the groundrules are readily accessible to every group member.

(Continued)

3. Keep them yourself and notice aloud if you break one.
4. Ensure that students keep their groundrules and if necessary, develop a set of consequences with the group for breaches of the rules.
5. Review the groundrules regularly to see if they still apply and to add any new ones that have become necessary.

Learning relationships

Research into learning has shown that the quality of relationships between learners and their teachers is the most important factor for increasing learning in a classroom (Deakin Crick et al., 2004). Interviews with students also indicate that they consider the relationship the class has with the teacher to be crucial to the success or failure of Circle Time. Research into learning suggests that the qualities of relationships that bring about most effective learning are those characterised by trust, affirmation and challenge. Trust is the characteristic that gives all parties confidence that the relationship can withstand the challenges of inequality, risk, uncertainty and difference. Some people want to set trust as a groundrule, but this is not possible. We can't legislate for people to trust one another. Rather this is a quality of relating that grows over a period of time. Developing an atmosphere where people can trust one another can only happen if people within the group prove themselves to be trustworthy. This is particularly true for the adults in the situation. They set the tone and, by their trustworthiness, facilitate the growth of trust in the wider group. Affirmation involves accepting other people as they are, without negative judgement or 'put-downs'. Once again, the adults in the circle model affirmation by the way in which they listen to the things that students say. Affirmation is demonstrated by taking each person's contribution seriously. Challenge means being stimulated to take the risks associated with learning, changing and growing, particularly in personal and social arenas where values, attitudes, beliefs and behaviours may be the subjects under challenge.

"In a circle, the teacher can talk to you more and make it interesting. You can say what you actually feel. The teacher is more our friend than our teacher. She isn't like any other normal teacher." (Student aged 13)

Implications for practice

Facilitating a circle requires self-knowledge on the part of the teacher. It depends on reflective self-awareness so that the adult is also growing and changing and is able to be self-consistent, true to her inner believing and valuing. The students said that *'To be successful, teachers need to be OK about themselves'*. Such teachers can create a respectful environment in which students respect each other and where good relationships develop between all members of the group.

"Circle Time gives the children more power. For some teachers this may be a problem. Although the teacher is still there she takes a back seat and becomes one of the group. So she loses a degree of power and control. Those who you think are quite insensitive suddenly come out and say something which totally changes your opinion. You see another side of their personality." (Taylor, 2003, p. 41).

Practical tips

1. Notice and give affirming eye contact to every member of the group.
2. Make sure that you listen and give respect to students' opinions, even if you disagree with them.
3. Get to know each student personally.
4. Take time for your own personal and professional growth.
5. Communicate your enjoyment of the students and your pleasure in being with them.

Teacher as role model

Humans learn by imitating people that they most admire and trust. The educational theorists call this mimetic learning. In a Circle Time session, the better the quality of the relationships that the teacher can establish in the group, the greater will be the mimetic learning. The teacher has a large measure of responsibility for both setting the tone in the circle session and modelling the beliefs, behaviours, attitudes and skills that the students need to be part of an effective, functioning group.

Teachers model in the circle by the way they respond to situations and to students and the way they tackle problems or difficulties. One of their primary tasks in the circle is to create a safe emotional climate so that students are able to make and admit mistakes and so learn from their own successes and failures and those of others, including the teacher's.

The students noted that they found it difficult if the teacher was embarrassed about a topic such as sex education. They were more caught up by the teacher's response than the subject matter. The teacher set the emotional tone. The teacher is the role model of the groundrules, the processes, listening, relationships and emotional tone.

> "We want to treat everyone else the way she treats us, like respect."
> (Student aged 13)

Implications for practice
Research into learning notes that modelling it is made up of a range of activities (Tew et al., 2004). These include making implicit ways of thinking explicit by talking about them. The teacher speaks his thoughts out loud and the students begin to understand how the teacher is thinking and the choices he is making. The teacher might say, 'I notice that there are some people who have a lot to say and some who are not getting heard. I suggest that we break into pairs so that everyone has a chance to speak and then we will bring some observations back to the circle.' In this way, the teacher models ways of including people and of giving voice to more silent or introverted personalities. He might become even more explicit and prefix the observation of vocal and non-vocal members of the group by validating difference. He might say, 'There are many different styles of communication and I notice that there are different styles in this group. I notice that some people …'. This method of voicing aloud internal thinking is a very helpful way of modelling inclusion and

affirmation of differences in the group. It can be used to demonstrate how to think about something and so make the hidden processes of thinking explicit to the student. Modelling can also be used to break a complex skill into its component parts so that each part is practised before building them back into a whole. This can be very helpful for a wide range of skills such as listening, problem solving, tackling a new task and so on. If the teacher can also model his own learning, students are reassured. The idea that we can all 'get it right' all, or even most of, the time is often unhelpful in a Circle Time setting. Adults who point out their mistakes or the ways in which they have modified what they are doing in response to the current situation, provide students with insights into the principles and concepts that lie beneath a new piece of learning, whether knowledge and factual understanding, skills, attitudes, values or beliefs.

Practical tips

1. Make it clear from the start that you are also a learner in the circle. This enables you to model your own learning and to learn from mistakes or unusual events that occur.
2. Become more aware of how much the students watch you and take their emotional and social lead from you.
3. Use students to model effective routines and procedures.
4. Think about skills that you want students to use such as listening or role play and break them down into smaller sub-skills so that students can learn them.
5. Give students time to reflect in pairs on what information or help they need in order to take part in the circle or to become proficient at a new skill.

Listening and dialogue

Circle Times build on the premise that a group is greater than the sum of its individual parts. It is therefore important that people listen to and appreciate the views of others. The word 'dialogue' is helpful here because it means a conversation in which each party listens and attends to the 'other'. Dialogue involves a quality of listening that affords the other parties the freedom and opportunity to examine their beliefs, values, attitudes and actions without fear of being judged, labelled or condemned. This is the quality of listening that counsellors use. It gives permission to think differently, to take risks and to try out new ideas and skills. One of the outcomes of dialogue is the challenge to change and develop as a person.

> "It doesn't matter what your opinion is. It is your opinion. We did a Circle Time on listening skills with 11- and 12-year-olds. Particularly the tutor group I've got are not good listeners at all and you could really see them at the end try to be active listeners, not shouting out." (PSHE teacher)

Implications for practice

The skills of active listening and dialogue are not natural. Anyone who has ever done any kind of counselling course will know that learning to listen well takes time, patience and practice. For students to function well in a circle, they need to explicitly learn the skills of active listening and taking part in a dialogue. Some schools introduce a listening course as part of their PSHE programme in Circle Time. Others have a course in listening that takes place outside the circle and then they bring the skills back into the circle. Whether the skills are learned during Circle Time, or in another context, students need to grow in self-awareness and master the range of skills that make up listening. They need to be able to recognise what it feels like when they are not listened to and recognise what it feels like to be listened to. They need to be able to identify the verbal and non-verbal evidence of when someone is listening and know the factors that make it easier and more difficult to listen to someone else. It is important to know what happens to your emotions when you disagree with someone else's point of view, recognise different tones of voice, know what they mean and recognise your response to them. They need to practise silently holding on to their thoughts while someone else finishes what they are saying. Perhaps most important is the need to be able to respectfully disagree with someone else's point of view and to separate a person from her opinion so that you don't take it personally.

1. Find a listening course that you can attend yourself.
2. Become familiar with the micro-skills that are involved in the skill we call active listening. These include non-verbal communication, facial expressions, open posture, eye contact and so on.
3. Talk about and teach the smaller skills before you expect students to be able to listen effectively or to take part in dialogues. It is important to practise the micro-skills a few at a time until students are self-aware enough to put them together into coherent big-scale skills that we call speaking and listening.
4. Use exercises in listening to raise students' self-awareness.
5. Become an active listener yourself and practise at home, in the staffroom, with friends, at the pub and anywhere else you can to increase your own skill level.

Controversial and sensitive issues

Topics of a controversial and sensitive nature fall into different categories. Almost any subject that is discussed in PSHE or in a circle can be controversial or sensitive for some members of the group. The older the studentsget, the more sensitive they become to perceived infringements of their privacy. On the other hand, there are some topics that are sensitive because they may elicit personal disclosures which put the teacher and the rest of the class in possession of sensitive information about students, some of it about illegal activity such as students, friends or relatives who are engaging in under-age sexual activity or using drugs. Teachers often fear this kind of disclosure in a circle context and avoid running circles so that it cannot happen.

"In a group I was covering for another teacher, we were talking about drugs and a girl started to talk about her sister who had been a heroin addict. She felt fine to talk about it and it really engaged the rest of the group. I was aware of the sensitive information this girl was giving out. She needed to talk about it but was perhaps not aware that all these other people were hearing it. She seemed to be OK to be talking about it. The rest of the group seemed to be quite shocked, though it was an event in the past. The group seemed to contain it well. I checked it out with the child protection officer in the school and it was well known to the senior staff in the school. After that I make it clear that in the circle I don't want them to use names. If they want to talk about things, they may want to come and see me privately rather than say it in the whole group." (PSHE teacher)

Implications for practice

The best way to avoid situations that place either teachers or students in compromising situations is to be clear about the rules of confidentiality which apply in these circumstances. The school should have a policy about confidentiality and guidance about who to go and see in particular instances. In Circle Time lessons, teachers should establish from the start that it may be inappropriate to disclose personal information. The groundrules should ensure that students agree not to pressure one another to answer questions about their own exprences.

"It would be better to have examples like Agony Aunts. As long as it isn't used too often it is really good. If they give them to groups of three people, at least one from the group can actually talk. Every group says something. You can hear people's views and they can give examples of what has happened if they feel like it." (Student aged 14)

Practical tips

1. Become familiar with the school's policy on confidentiality. (If there isn't one, ask for it to be written, or offer to do it.)
2. Make sure you know which members of senior staff are responsible for child protection issues and what issues fall within their remit.
3. Make and enforce groundrules with the students to protect them from gossip outside the group, including taking the information home.
4. Make yourself available for one-to-one chats so that students do not have to use the circle forum to talk about personal matters.

(Continued)

5. Use a range of techniques during Circle Time that support personal discussion without you hearing it such as: paired or small groupwork; distancing techniques such as Agony Aunts, hypothetical case studies, role play and anonymous suggestions in a hat. These will ensure that issues can be explored without the need for personal disclosure.

Professional learning buddies

Time and time again in interviews with staff, people mentioned the need for someone to learn alongside. Staff reported feeling a sense of isolation which was unhelpful when acquiring a new way of working such as Circle Time. Staff said that they would value a colleague with whom to discuss circle sessions, brainstorm alternative approaches including the use of language in the circle and exchange ideas for games and activities. They also wanted someone with whom they could confidentially debrief difficult situations and events and confer over issues that arose.

> "I learnt by using the secondary Circle Time book [Mosely and Tew, 1998] and by basically asking people who are experienced."
> "I was observed teaching and team taught a Circle Time lesson." (PSHE teachers)

Implications for practice

Our interviews revealed that some staff make their own opportunities for professional learning but would like their learning to be more formally supported through the structures and systems of the school. On the other hand, the students are very concerned that they should not be the subject of discussion in the staffroom or between members of staff. One of their fears about talking in a meaningful way in the circle is that they would become the subject of staff discussion.

> "We're concerned about teachers talking about our stuff in the staffroom." (Student aged 14)

34

If students are to feel safe that teachers have a learning buddy that they talk to about running circles, then they need to know that the same rules of confidentiality would apply to the teachers as to the students. The teachers would need to talk about issues and not individuals. They would have to avoid the use of names and protect the privacy of the students.

Practical tips

1. Make an agreement with a colleague to be learning buddies to one another.
2. Set up a regular time when you each get a chance to talk about your Circle Time experiences.
3. Ensure that you observe the same groundrules of confidentiality that you agree with the students and separate names from issues.
4. Debrief the events and issues of Circle Time and make sure that you always come away with a new way forward. Avoid turning this into a moan session. Make it a learning experience.
5. Try keeping a learning journal about your experiences and look back at the progress you have made at the end of the year.

Section Three

Implementing Circle Time

The structure of a Circle Time session

Effective Circle Time is a group process that pays attention to the ways in which groups form, function, cope with conflict, perform tasks and close. It is considerably more than sitting the class in a circle to talk.

A Circle Time session is planned so that each time the group meets, there is an opportunity for the individuals to come together and form (or re-form) themselves into a cohesive group. This formation phase is followed by an opportunity to engage with an issue or a task and the session ends with time to disengage from the group before moving on to the next part of the school day.

In summary, the Circle Time structure has three sections:

- *beginning phase* when the group reconvenes
- *middle phase* when the group performs a task and/or considers an issue. In this phase the class group functions using ways of working together that they have discussed and agreed in previous sessions. Every circle meeting provides an opportunity to refine and develop these ways of working, however, including time to develop strategies for dealing with any conflicts that may arise
- *closing phase* when the group terminates this session.

Beginning phase

At the beginning of any group session, it is important to allocate time to allaying the anxieties of the group and to finding some connection between group members. Virtually everyone enters a group situation with a host of anxieties that often lie outside of direct awareness, but affect behaviour. Consider how we feel as adults when we go to a party where we don't know the other guests or attend a professional course as the only person from our school. The less familiar the group is with each other, the higher the anxiety. People's anxiety is an expression of their internal uncertainty around issues such as:

▶ Will others like me?
▶ Will I tell too much about myself?
▶ Will people talk about me outside the group?
▶ What if people laugh and make fun of me?

It is vital that the atmosphere of the PSHE or Citizenship lesson starts positively. However much you may feel like shouting or disciplining the students, make every effort to tactically ignore the problem students and concentrate on praising those, usually the vast majority, who are doing well. Merely smiling and thanking individual students can have a transforming effect on the pupils who are seeking attention by acting out. Sometimes it helps to stand near any potential disruptors and smile at them or even touch them lightly on the arm to show you're there! Try to highlight those who are being good, even for a second, and show surprise, not anger, if they act out. That way you are showing them that you expect them to behave well because you know they can and will!

In circles a game is often the quickest way to bring the group together, allay anxiety and create a positive atmosphere. Students of all ages report enjoying games, particularly if the teacher is also visibly enjoying it and if there is some choice and control over how the game is played. Games work best when they are fun and also related to a topic or issue that is the subject of discussion for this session. For instance, trust games can introduce a discussion of safety, of risk and certainty, or co-operative games can be used to introduce a session when the subject under discussion is working together or when the task requires co-operative working.

> "The worst part of the lesson is when you first go in before you start moving around in the warm-up activity. If there was no ice-breaker, it would be much more difficult."

"We play fun games that are interactive and everyone laughs. We have to get more confident with one another in the games. We sit next to different people and it is good." (Students aged 12)

Before starting, it is best to set the chairs out in the best circle you can manage in the space. It is important that the students can see everyone and that you can see all of them. Any disruptive students may well gravitate to the sides or places where you cannot see them, so making the best circle you can from the very start is essential. It is also vital that you use chairs of the same size. If you use a mixture of chairs, then the computer chairs, or the padded teacher's chair, will be the ones that everyone goes for in the games. The only exception to this rule is if you have students with adapted chairs for particular needs. Space is always a problem in secondary schools, but if you possibly can, beg the use of the drama studio, a carpeted large room, or one where you can move furniture without too much noise or fuss. Do try to avoid a 'goldfish bowl' room like the dining hall, especially just before or after lunch. There is nothing worse than having complaints about chairs scraping or noisy games being played by teachers trying to run silent tests below or above you!

Do not allow anyone to sit outside the circle unless this is specifically agreed. For instance, a pupil with special educational needs (SEN) may need to watch with a Learning Support Assistant (LSA) before he feels confident enough to join in. The point of insisting that everyone sits in the circle is so that you can see all the students' faces and they can see you. Reading body language is important but try to ignore any student who is deliberately trying to wind you up. A handy technique is to quickly swap places with a troublesome student, or you may ask him to do you a favour or an errand. 'Could you pop over and close the window, please James? Thanks, you did that brilliantly, a merit mark for you if you carry on so well!' When James returns, his seat is elsewhere because you have popped into it while he was helping you.

The circle is a good place to notice and praise the skills of learning. With secondary students it is important not to seem patronising. Yet praising a student's concentration and setting them up as a perfect example, possibly backed up with a credit, can transform individuals and give them a new label such as 'particularly skilled in concentration'. One favourite is to point out a student's fantastic looking skills, then make a joke by saying, 'Great Sam, you're not only good at looking, but you're good-looking too!'

Implications for practice

At the beginning of any group session it is really important to allay fears, bring the group together and re-establish the ways of working together. Games and ice-breaker activities are one of the quickest and simplest ways of reconvening the group. The fifth section of this book provides a selection of games and activities that can be used at the beginning of a Circle Time session to:

▶ produce connection between group members
▶ create laughter to release the tension generated by anxiety
▶ introduce the topic or theme of the lesson
▶ raise emotions that might be the subject of the lesson
▶ bring students into the group in an experiential way.

Practical tips

1. Learn games so that you can draw from a good repertoire.
2. Practise games with any group of friends (or colleagues) before trying them on classes of students. Some staff use them at the beginning of staff meetings.
3. Make sure students become very familiar with one another (names, hobbies, safe personal information, interests and so on).
4. Get students to teach you games and/or lead them.
5. Think about ice-breaker activities other than games that you could use, such as paired discussions, shared histories, music, photographs that trigger thoughts and/or feelings.

Middle phase

This part of the circle session is when the group task is done. It might involve acquisition of knowledge and understanding relating to some aspect of the PSHE and Citizenship curricula such as the examination of personal and/or societal values and attitudes or the opportunity to practise skills. A group cannot function well in performing a task until it has established productive ways of working. At this stage, any residual anxiety will result in passive, aggressive or withdrawn patterns of behaviour. These ways of behaving serve the purpose of helping individuals deal with their anxieties, but they also cut them off from the possibility of connecting to others in ways that would more productively reduce anxiety. Once cycles of aggression or withdrawal are in place, they become difficult to break and individuals find it increasingly hard to escape from their patterns of behaviour to engage with the group in more productive ways.

The art is to recognise withdrawn or aggressive behaviour as a symptom of a deeper need rather than a personalised threat to discipline or classroom management. Once we recognise these behaviours as distancing techniques that serve a safety function for the individual, it is easier to rise to the challenge of providing a relationship, group structures and activities that create an atmosphere of trust and connection which in turn should produce enjoyment. For instance, if the group behaviour indicates that several people do not feel safe in the larger group, discussion can be broken down into pairs or smaller groups so that personal views are considered in the safety of a small context before anything is said in the larger and more frightening arena of the whole-class circle.

It is common practice in Circle Time to have a 'round' so that students are given an opportunity to speak and voice their opinion, for example 'One thing I am afraid of is . . .'

During student interviews, some students said that they tended to play very safe during rounds. At first they only expressed opinions that they thought would be acceptable in the group (either to the teacher or to their peers). They confessed to making something up rather than giving their honest opinion and thereby running the risk of ridicule in the group.

"Before we had Circle Time everyone laughed at one another. Now we've started to respect each other because the teacher has taught us to let people have their opinion."

"Over time this year, we have learned to trust each other and we can now take part." (Students aged 14)

Implications for practice

Teachers said that some students chose to pass and say nothing rather than voice a view that might be ridiculed in the group. They said that only when groundrules were agreed and enforced in a meaningful way did ridicule, unkind laughter and put-downs stop. Once the group was seen to be a safe place, honest opinions and perceptions became more common and the round became a meaningful exchange of views and opinions, connected to real feelings. The teachers said that once this happened it became possible to explore, challenge and even change opinions, values and attitudes.

Practical tips

1. Think about changing the groups regularly so that the students do not always work in a whole circle. There are more opportunities to talk in pairs or small groups of three or four.
2. Do not always ask students to work with people they don't know well. We all need safety before we can talk about very personal things. Think about the subject under discussion and decide whether friendship groups or non-friendship groups would be the more appropriate.
3. Only have one or two rounds during a circle session and always use a sentence stem so that people know how to begin what they want to say, for example 'We think lunchtimes would be better if . . . '.
4. Always have an alternative activity in case the one you planned does not work well. Alternative scenarios relevant to the topic under discussion for the group to enact or discuss are a good safeguard.
5. Think about different learning styles and cater for the kinaesthetic, the auditory and the visual learners during a circle session.

Closing phase

The end of each session involves breaking the close bonds that develop during an effective group session. Inevitably this results in a loss of emotional energy and can be accompanied by increased levels of anxiety. It is good to remember that anxiety is allayed if there is the certain knowledge of a similarly good time together next week. The art here is to provide activities and routines that reduce anxiety and bring a sense of closure. It is often helpful to reflect on previous experiences – to recall things that have gone well and previous satisfactory outcomes. Sometimes students can practise giving and receiving affirming feedback to one another. It can also help to close the lesson with a game or activity that reunites the group and relieves any tension by providing an opportunity to laugh. One teacher we interviewed said that he ends each PSHE and Citizenship lesson in a circle with a reminder of things that have gone well and a focus on achievement and success. Teachers or students will often introduce a game that generates laughter and brings emotional closure to the topic that has been discussed. Favourite games involve some element of detection such as Wink Sleep where the 'murderer' has to be discovered or Where's the Object? (Page 123).

> "We like Circle Time but it needs variety to make it interesting like new games and activities. We love the games. You need them to start it off. It needs pace too. Not too slow." (Student aged 14)

Implications for practice

When a Circle Time session finishes with a sense of completion, it leaves students looking forward to the next session. The lesson needs to end on a positive and up-beat note so that any raw emotions raised by the issues discussed in the lesson are closed down again. If the subject matter of the PSHE lesson has been difficult, sensitive or controversial, then it helps to end on laughter and a lighter note. If the lesson was very active and high in energy, it helps to end on a calm activity so that the students leave in a composed frame of mind. It is also worth thinking about where the students will be going next lesson and providing some kind of bridge between the circle and the next part of the day.

1. Think of your Circle Time lesson as five or more minutes shorter than it actually is so that you have time for a good finishing activity and reordering the room.
2. Have a range of closing activities or games to hand so that you can select one according to the mood of the class at the end of the lesson.
3. Make sure that you know at least one calming activity and one that will make the class laugh.
4. Take time to reflect on good experiences, positive outcomes and student successes so that the last thing the students remember is an affirming experience.
5. Develop a good routine with the class for putting the room back into order so that the lesson does not end on a mad scramble after the bell has gone.

Circle Time routines

Circle Time routines are a range of processes that Circle Time practitioners have found enable the circle to run effectively. Every class that uses Circle Time regularly has to learn the skills and routines of the circle. As with any set of skills, Circle Time routines only become second nature to the students with constant repetition and practice. Embedding Circle Time processes and procedures takes time and once they are established, the group is able to function effectively. This is the equivalent of Tuckman's (1973) norming. Circle Time routines involve establishing expectations of 'the way we do things round here'. These might include students working with any of the other students in the class, not just with their best friends. It is important to agree with students how they will signal that they want to speak during open discussion. In most classrooms, students put their hands up before they speak, but other signals can be devised if the group wishes.

Most models of Circle Time involve some kind of round. This is the opportunity for everyone to speak at least once during the circle session. During a round each person can choose to contribute an opinion, factual information or experience. On the other hand, no individual is forced to speak and anyone can choose to pass. Rounds can become very boring if there are too many during a session or if each student can speak for an unspecified length of time. The best way to keep the round paced is to introduce a sentence stem that each student finishes with her own perspective or experience. Sometimes it is appropriate for pairs to answer together, reducing the number of responses to 15 rather than 30. Some Circle Time practitioners use a speaking object that is passed round the circle to signal a person's turn to speak; others trust to the self-control of the group members and each person takes a turn without any visual symbol.

No matter what topic is being discussed, an important feature of Circle Time is keeping a good pace so that the circle does not become boring. The most skilled Circle Time facilitators always have a range of activities that they could introduce if the pace slows or students show evidence of disengagement or boredom. Many of the activities might not be used but they are 'on hand' ready. It helps to incorporate 'brain breaks' and changes in activity during the circle. Interest and energy are sustained by regular changes in pace and activity, particularly when these involve all learning styles (visual, auditory and kinaesthetic).

Implications for practice
Perhaps the most important routine of Circle Time is the skill of active listening. It is something that all of us, students and adults alike, need to learn and practise. The most common confusion is the difference between hearing and listening. Students who become skilled at Circle Time processes learn to attend to the speaker while simultaneously attending to their own internal responses. Skilled listening is a precursor to developing empathy.

Training sessions can involve learning and practising a range of activities in different learning styles and matching them to a variety of learning outcomes.

"My 15-year-olds are the most resistant to Circle Time, but when they are sat in class in the conventional way, they are not good at listening. When they are sat in the circle, at least they are not talking to one another. When we have done Circle Time, I feel more people have contributed that way than when we have done lessons sat at their desks." (PSHE teacher)

Practical tips

1. Agree with your students at the beginning of the year the routines that you will use during Circle Time such as whether they will sit boy girl at the beginning of the Circle Time or how they will indicate that they want to speak during Circle Time.
2. Agree with older students whether they want to use a speaking object or not. If they decide to use one, discuss which object the group will use.
3. Make sure you know a range of brain gym activities (Hannaford, 1994) so that you refocus the group when attention wanders.
4. Try to remain flexible about the lesson content. Sometimes it is more productive to abandon the planned subject matter and 'go with' the issues that are present in the group at the moment.
5. Make it a policy that any failure to use the agreed routines will become the subject of group discussion – ask the group what should happen next.

The whole circle versus paired work and smaller groups

In primary schools, Circle Time is most often run as a whole-class activity. The class remains as a complete group for the half-hour session. Games, activities, discussion and problem solving all take place in the centre of the circle with all members of the class taking part. In secondary schools, particularly when Circle Time is used for discussing topics as part of the PSHE or Citizenship curricula, the whole circle is not always the best forum to use for the entire lesson or for every aspect of all subjects. Pairs and small groups are useful in secondary schools for a number of reasons. They make sure that everyone gets an opportunity to talk without having to listen to all the views. They also ensure that there is a chance to talk about issues confidentially in a small group or with one other person without having to disclose information to the teacher. This is particularly important for adolescent young people who are acutely aware of child protection issues and of potential adult disapproval of their activities. The smaller groupings ensure the lesson keeps a good pace fh as many people actively engaged as possible.

Teachers of PSHE and Citizenship need to develop a repertoire of groupwork skills and plan lessons to use a range of group sizes from whole circle to pairs, threes, fours and so on. It is, however, always good to begin in the circle and return to the circle at the end of the lesson.

> "Often paired discussion is quite good then I ask them what their pair thinks. Often I will restrict them to just two things so that they don't have to think up endless things. They don't all have to say something but can say 'This is what our group thinks'. I am quite conscious that they feel a little bit less exposed." (PSHE teacher)

Implications for practice
Many activities can be conducted in the whole circle, but more sensitive subjects are better discussed in smaller, safer contexts with carefully selected information being fed back to the whole group. This raises the question of group composition. Teachers are encouraged to use their professional judgement about when to use friendship groups and when to mix the groups up and require students to work with other, less familiar members of the class group.

> "You are far more productive with your friends."
> "You need the opportunity to get to know other people but not bunged in with someone and told you have five minutes to do this piece of work. You need time to find out who they actually are before you can work with them." (Students aged 14)

Sometimes, PSHE and Citizenship lessons require some written work such as a lifeline, making a poster or recording reflections in notebooks or journals. If the writing is minimal, it is possible to do it while still in the circle. Clipboards can be useful for this kind of work, or an investment in chairs with fold-back desks attached to the arm. If the written work is more extensive, the use of a circle might not be relevant that week. The circle is most useful for discussion about factual information and/or examining opinions, views, attitudes and values.

Practical tips

1. Consider what format is most suited to the lesson content when planning.
2. Try to ring the changes between whole circle, paired and small group work and consider friendship, non-friendship, gender, ability, random and interest groupings.
3. If written work is going to take up most of the lesson, try placing the desks around the outside of the room and putting the chairs inside them. Turn the chairs to face in for the circle discussion and out so that students have a desk for written work.
4. Consider the use of clipboards or special chairs for small amounts of written work.
5. Remember to review these issues with the students and get their feedback on what works best for them.

Writing a Circle Time lesson plan

Schools that adopt a Circle Time approach for PSHE and Citizenship often adapt their programmes of study and lesson plans so that the lessons can be delivered as Circle Time sessions or as more conventional lessons. Indeed it is necessary to have conventional lessons available for when supply teachers cover the class. It is useful to give staff the opportunity during training time to select topics from the schemes of work and practise turning them into circle sessions. The first step is to identify the desired learning outcomes of the lesson and choose appropriate opening activities for the beginning phase of the Circle Time. Next, decide on the main subject of the lesson in terms of the knowledge and understanding, values, attitudes or skills that are involved. The activities in the middle phase of the lesson plan include:

resource information; informed discussion about the topic; revision quizzes; visual material such as video clips, photographs and artefacts; role-play scenarios; hypothetical case studies; open discussion; values continua; rounds; and the hosting of a visiting expert. It is important when planning a lesson to ensure time is given for reflection and review of the learning. Good practice includes having a closing phase which provides time for review of the lesson, an opportunity to focus on some successes, and a game or activity that finishes the topic and brings the group back together. (Some examples of PSHE and Citizenship lessons written as circle scripts are given in Section Four.)

One teacher wrote about a lesson on disability that she ran. Students were encouraged to consider what it feels like to be disabled, their attitudes and reactions to disability and how they might deal with disability for themselves and in other people. As part of this work, students simulate disabilities such as sensory impairments. They then have to negotiate the school with a partner without using the disabled sense. This exercise requires a high level of trust between student pairs. The following week, a circle session was used to facilitate reflection on the experience and to look at personal and societal values, attitudes and behaviours towards disability. Teachers were encouraged to use a trust game, such as a blindfolded guided walk or getting the whole group to sit on one another's laps in a tight circle without falling over, in the opening phase of Circle Time to introduce the discussion.

Implications for practice
Not all PSHE or Citizenship topics are best suited to a Circle Time session. Interviews with teachers revealed a tension between lessons that were very knowledge based and those that were more oriented towards exploration of values, attitudes and opinions. The former were not always best suited to a circle, though it was felt that beginning in a circle and ending in a circle was always a preferred way of working if the physical space in the room could easily accommodate it.

Another tension that appeared during the interviews was the place of written work and its relationship to the circle. This has already been touched on in the section on 'Whole circle versus paired work and smaller groups'. The students' view on written work in the circle was summed up by one of them as follow

"We can have good discussions and go around getting everyone's point of view. The circle is good for discussing because you can see everybody and you feel like you want to say something. If you want to do written work, the circle is not the best place because you can distract other people and you don't have anywhere to write. If the aim of the lesson is to discuss, then we should be in the circle the whole time. If we are working on other things, then you should maybe be at your desk." (Student aged 15)

This seems to be, once again, a matter of professional judgement. However, if a school is committed to using the circle, there is an argument for making more appropriate furniture or space available to make it easier to run. Specialist spaces and equipment are available for many other subjects such as science, drama, technology, to name a few; why not for PSHE and active Citizenship?

Practical tips

1. Practise changing conventional PSHE and Citizenship lessons into Circle Time sessions.
2. Make sure you have the lesson plan well in advance of the lesson rather than on the same morning.
3. Look at the learning outcomes and decide if the circle is the best format for achieving them.
4. Spend some time in the space you have available for your lesson and work out the quickest and most efficient way to rearrange the furniture to get a good circle.
5. Don't try to force a writing-based lesson into a circle format. Have two sessions – one for the written work and one for the discussion to apply the knowledge or discuss the attitudes, values and beliefs.

The place of learning outcomes in Circle Time

Citizenship and PSHE have different status from one another in the National Curriculum for England and Wales. Citizenship is a foundation subject in the National Curriculum and therefore has a statutory programme of study for students aged 11–16. The programme of study includes knowledge, skills and understanding about becoming informed citizens, developing skills of enquiry and communication and developing skills of participation and responsible action. PSHE, on the other hand, is not a statutory National Curriculum subject. There is no programme of study. Non-statutory guidelines cover three strands: developing confidence and responsibility and making the most of their abilities; developing a healthy, safer lifestyle; developing good relationships and respecting the differences between people. These strands are underpinned by a recommended breadth of opportunity.

PASSPORT (Lees and Plant, 2000) is a very useful publication. This booklet draws together all the subject matter that relates to students' personal and social development whether it comes from the Citizenship programme of study or from the PSHE framework and creates a menu of learning outcomes. Schools are encouraged to go through a consultation exercise with students, staff, parents and governors to decide which areas are of importance and relevance to their context alongside statutory elements such as sex and relationships and careers education. The use of learning outcomes makes lesson planning much easier, though in a circle session (or indeed any PSHE lesson) staff need the flexibility to change the direction of a lesson in response to the needs and interests of the group.

> "It is sensible to have a curriculum. But some subjects we do every year the same over again. We went over in the first year of secondary school things we had already done in primary school. When we were 9 and 10 we did puberty and then we did it again when we were 11 and again when we were 12 or 13." (Student aged 14)

Implications for practice
In PSHE it seems to be important to have a more flexible approach to the curriculum, lesson content and learning outcomes. The students really appreciated a teacher's ability to change direction from the planned lesson in order to help sort out an issue that was going on in the group and seriously impairing the quality of learning.

"We had an experience that wasn't a nice experience, but it was a productive experience. Everyone was saying what they thought about an issue. Some people may have cried but things were sorted out during that lesson. A question was asked: How did the teacher manage the difficult subject? She let us get on with it and helped us discuss it." (Student aged 15)

Practical tips

1. Have clear learning outcomes and a good sense of what you want to achieve in the lesson.
2. Match the lesson content and process to the learning outcomes.
3. If the lesson is taking a different direction, take a risk and go with it. See what happens.
4. Reflect on your Circle Time lessons with a friend or colleague and see if you can find more helpful approaches or language for achieving learning outcomes.
5. Always look for a moment of success when you reflect on a lesson and don't get caught in the trap of focusing exclusively on the difficult parts or failures.

Watching a demonstration circle

The old adage says 'Tell me, I forget. Show me, I remember. Involve me, I understand.' Consequently, one of the most powerful ways of learning to run circle sessions is to watch a more experienced colleague or a trainer run one, or better still, co-run one. Demonstration circles work best when they take a PSHE lesson and are as close to 'reality' as possible. For example, a demonstration lesson could be 50 minutes long with a full class of thirty 11- and 12-year-olds. Staff watch the circle and then have a good half-hour in which to reflect on their observations and consider the implications for their own practice.

Watching a colleague or another professional work with students that are familiar to you is very revealing. Seeing a different approach, noting the use of language, watching how the subject matter is tackled are all helpful in stimulating greater professional self-awareness. Staff are often very willing to apply the experientially 'felt' learning gained through observation in their own practice.

One opportunity to observe a Circle Time lesson is not enough for ongoing professional development, however. Staff often express a need and desire for continuing opportunities to observe or work with more experienced colleagues.

> "It would be nice to develop the training further. Most people have got the basic training and are able to step it up so we can work through problems with more experienced people and share practice." (Head of Year)

Implications for practice

Making the time available for in-house continuing professional development is both sought after by staff and rewarding in the improvements that it yields. Teachers often feel a sense of isolation. They have few reference points for making judgements about their own performance in any teaching situation and these are particularly relevant when acquiring a new way of working with its accompanying skill set. They are looking for opportunities to discuss their work, to debrief difficult events and to watch more experienced colleagues. They are very grateful when sympathetic senior management release them to observe a colleague or co-facilitate a group with them. This is particularly appreciated when there is an opportunity to benefit from the expertise of senior staff in a non-judgemental and developmental way.

Practical tips

1. Make sure that you have an opportunity to attend Circle Time training where there is a demonstration circle.
2. Take time (even by using a free period) to watch a more experienced colleague run a circle session.
3. Ask for an experience of co-facilitating a circle either with a peer or a more senior colleague.
4. Take time to reflect on your circle observation and note the things you saw that would enhance your own practice.

(Continued)

5. Notice that there is no such thing as a perfect Circle Time and remember to be kind to yourself next time you evaluate your performance in a negative way.

Managing the set up and set down of the circle

Both staff and students note the difficulty of setting up the room for lessons run in a circle format. Some classrooms in secondary schools have special functions such as art rooms and science laboratories; some are too small or contain too much additional furniture to accommodate a good circle of at least 25 and often more than 30 chairs. The physical constraints of the space can become a serious disincentive to running circles, particularly if the lessons are shorter than an hour. PSHE and Citizenship specialists also usually teach another subject such as PE, religious education (RE) or history. This means that they have to get from a sports changing room to a conventional classroom at the start of the lesson and unlock the door to let the students in before the room can be rearranged into a circle.

"It is difficult setting up the room and it would be nicer if there were rooms set up already for you. Even if you do set up the room you are disturbing classes all around you. You lose time and have to put it back at the end and it looks messy with furniture at the side." (PSHE teacher)

Implications for practice

Schools that have the most success at embedding Circle Time practice give considerable thought to the issues of setting up and setting down the circle in a teaching room. This can be time consuming, noisy to colleagues in adjacent rooms and disturbing to the class, making it difficult to re-establish a calm, productive working atmosphere. Some secondary schools that run regular Circle Time have one or two spaces that are always set up as a circle, such as a space in the library suite, or next to the drama studio. Where lack of teaching space is an issue, this is not possible and alternative strategies include setting the desks around the walls of the teaching room so that the students face out to write and in for the circle. This works particularly well for teaching spaces used for English, where speaking and listening are core parts of the curriculum. Schools can also invest in chairs that have small desks attached to the arms or use the end of science labs and art spaces (though sitting for an hour on a stool is not very comfortable or practical).

Practical tips

1. Try different approaches to setting up the room and see which works best with your students.
2. Discuss the set up with the students and take their advice on the best way forward.
3. Have a rotating team for setting up the room. They report to you on the morning of the PHSE lesson to find out whether a circle is needed or not and are responsible for getting the room unlocked and ready at the beginning of the lesson. (It could be done during break or at the end of lunchtime if the lesson follows either.)
4. If you use the whole class for set up and set down, make this part of the learning at the beginning of the year so there is a military procedure for it. Number the desks, have a plan on the wall, decide on an order for moving furniture and practise. (Do make sure that you consider the health and safety policy of your school when moving furniture.)
5. Take the issue to faculty meetings so that representation is made to senior management. This is an important subject area and it needs as much consideration as any other.

The role of games in Circle Time

"You can learn more about a person in an hour of play than in a year of conversation." (Plato 428–348 bc)

Games are conventionally used in the beginning phase of Circle Time in order to bring the group together. There is no reason why games cannot be played at any point in the circle lesson, however, and they are very useful in the closing phase to bring the circle to an end. They perform many functions including refocusing the sense of 'group', lightening the mood, providing a 'brain break' or creating a 'felt' experience of a topic under discussion.

In secondary schools staff are often reluctant to use games. They perceive them to be a waste of precious curriculum time, or childish. Similarly, students can be scathing about games and feel that they are being patronised or treated as children, particularly between the ages of 14 and 16. It should be noted that from 16 to 18, students become more relaxed about themselves and are willing to join in games with as much enthusiasm as they did when they were young.

The key to successful games seems to lie in the teacher's conviction that this is a meaningful and purposeful activity. The member of staff should be clear about the learning that is intrinsic to the game, the reason he chose to use this particular game and the way he will connect the game to the topic under discussion. When students perceive an activity to be relevant and useful, they are more willing to take part in it, even if it might cause them a certain amount of embarrassment. Similarly, the member of staff must be willing to play the game with as much enthusiasm as he expects from the students. Engagement in the game is modelled by the adult and imitated by the students. In any case, most people find games fun and far preferable to worksheets.

One of the problems teachers report is that they run out of ideas for games and students may become bored if the same activities are run too often. Section Five gives an extensive range of games that you can use with secondary aged students.

All the games use the skills for learning. Good practice is to remind students of these skills by noticing and appreciating them as the game progresses. It is really important, however, that all appreciation and praise are genuine and not seen as empty or too sugary. Students can always tell whether teachers are being genuine or false in their use of praise. They do like being noticed though, especially as most teachers never notice the quiet, well-behaved students because they are too busy looking out for those who grab their attention!

There are many games to play and the broader your repertoire the better. However, the way you play them is important to the overall success of your lesson. The most important thing is to plan carefully so that you can tie in the learning from the game you play with the learning outcomes of the lesson. The games should feel like an intrinsic part of the lesson as they naturally lead into a round or discussion. It is therefore important to choose the games that will give the students the learning experience you want.

Many teachers report their nervousness at running games which may seem 'babyish' for their 'sophisticated' group. We have found that if you are quite OK and relaxed with the fact that the lesson will be fun and games are a better alternative to worksheets, things will go well. Talk to your drama teachers. They play games all the time. Some students may feel that some activities are exclusive to drama, but if you have done your research, you can say, 'I know you can play this one brilliantly because you play it in drama with Mrs X'. The main key to successful games is not to falter. Those steely stares or sneers from the students who try to show they are too old for this sort of stuff can be overtaken by the fun enjoyed by the bulk of the tutor set or group. If you have support staff in the lesson, get them on your side and encourage them to share and take some responsibility for games or the running of the circle.

"I don't think it's what the game is. I think some people don't want to stand out by doing anything in a game that would make them stand out, so they'd rather not do any games." (Student aged 14)

"We play fun games that are interactive and everyone laughs. We have to get more confident with one another in the games. There isn't anyone in the group who never speaks." (Student aged 13)

Implications for practice
Teachers who use Circle Time most successfully become comfortable and confident with games and activities that require some self-disclosure. Not all teachers want to do this, and it is probably better that those who can't or won't reveal something of themselves avoid teaching PSHE, particularly in a circle. We are asking students to consider their values, attitudes and behaviour,

to look at sensitive topics and emotive issues. It seems only reasonable to suggest that staff who lead such activities should be willing to examine their own attitudes and values so that they are also learners in the PSHE lesson. One teacher's observation was: "I found that my relationship with my tutor set improved when I started to talk about myself in a more open way."

Practical tips

1. Remember that students 'read' our attitudes towards them. Reflect on how much you enjoy being with students and whether you convey that in your PSHE lessons.
2. Find a level of activity that you are comfortable with and give it all of yourself. You don't have to be 'bubbly' all of the time, but you do need to be congruent.
3. Try a range of games and activities with a group. If they won't join in, make this the subject of discussion for a Circle Time session and find out where the difficulty lies.
4. Explain to the students the purpose of the game that you have planned and if they are not comfortable with it, can they think of an equally good and acceptable way of introducing the lesson?
5. Connect the games to social situations that students will be familiar with so that they can see the relevance and importance of practising these skills.

Frequently asked questions about Circle Time

Q: Some of my students always try to sit outside the circle so that they are hiding and I cannot see them. We are restricted for space, but they always seem to find a corner to hide in.

A: It is really important to have the most circular circle you can, on chairs of the same height and size. Do not start the lesson until all the students are present and you can see everyone's face and body clearly. Any reluctant participants should be praised and encouraged to move into the circle before you start. Re-form the circle after very active games so that you can see everyone and they can see you. You can, if really pushed, run a circle lesson with tables in the middle, but it stops you moving the students easily and can mean that you are restricted in what you can achieve in terms of groupwork and moving students around physically.

Q: There are always a few dominant personalities in my groups who 'Pass' in every round. Their influence is such that very few others speak so it becomes very dull. Help please!

A: First, split them up by playing some Mixing games so that the challenging students are split from their cliques. Secondly, praise them at every opportunity to motivate them to come on board. Thirdly, use paired discussion before you initiate a round so that you can check every pair has something to say and everyone has a chance to chat through their ideas quietly before sharing them. Lastly, have a word with these students out of class time to enhance your relationship with them and make them feel special to you. Sometimes you can prime them by explaining what you are going to discuss in the next circle and praise their thoughtfulness or comments from last time.

Q: How do I stop students breaking out into chat when someone else is speaking? I try to use the speaking object but they don't seem to respect it, so I feel out of control.

A: One of the delights of circle teaching is that you can split students into pairs or small groups to allow them to chat ideas through before they share them with the larger group. We all like to respond and air our thoughts, and it is very important to note that you don't have to stay in a circle but can spilt into pairs, small groups or whatever suits. Often there is no need to reconvene to feed back, so any points made can be jotted down or used for reflection, an extension task or homework. Make rounds brief and snappy by: pairing students up so you only have 15 utterances; by using a script so students merely complete a short sentence; by giving plenty of opportunity for pairs or foursomes to talk in small groups. These strategies help students to be quiet and listen to others because they know their turn will come. Having well-known groundrules before you start is important so that mutual respect, no put-downs and a generally positive feel to the lesson are maintained. This is why you as facilitator need to be energised, positive, well prepared and ready for fun before the session starts. It is worth noting here that some teachers dislike using a speaking object and this is entirely up to you and your group. Try without it, but reintroduce it if you feel they need it as a signal for permission to speak and be heard. Never let students speak while others whisper or chat. The atmosphere of mutual respect will be lost and the message given is that what is being said is not important.

Q: Aren't the games too babyish for my students? I feel embarrassed that they might rebel and refuse to play.

A: Your enthusiasm and certainty that the games and circle will go well are key here. These students play games in PE and drama and they almost certainly would prefer to play games than do worksheets, so give it a go! With difficult groups, it might help to whisper that some of the games are pub drinking games so you are reluctant to teach them. That usually does the trick!

Q: I know that my group want to have a circle lesson, but I'm afraid of losing control. I know that there are a couple of saboteurs waiting to run riot or ruin the lesson and it makes me too afraid to try. Help!

A: You are not alone in feeling this way! Many teachers worry about changing their role to become more facilitative rather than didactic. I usually say that if you have some really difficult saboteurs in the group, have a supporter in with you the first time. Maybe the Head of PSHE or a member of the SMT would join you. This becomes someone who can help you to remove students if the need arises. Support from senior personnel is in addition to any LSAs who may be there supporting specific students. If you have other adults in the circle, make sure that they obey the groundrules and don't talk while you or another student is talking. It is a really good idea to have a copy of the lesson script for adult supporters. The hope is that, in time, they may feel confident enough to run some of the activities or games.

An alternative to asking for support in your circle is to remove the really serious potential disruptors. These will probably be those on the school's register of special needs for emotional and behavioural difficulties (EBD), or those who have been suspended a number of times. You need only remove them for the first few lessons, so that the group gels well and trust is established. They can then be reintroduced one at a time, on a behaviour contract. In this way, the group's cohesive force should overcome any individual attempts at rebellion. This has to be handled very sensitively, remembering that the ultimate aim is to include all students. Sometimes we have to be pragmatic, however, in order to get a new way of working off the ground. Including challenging students isn't easy and you can't really allow them to opt out. After all, they can't opt out of other activities in the curriculum, so they need to know that they are expected to take part. It is easy to make the mistake of allowing students to opt out only to find you have half the class refusing to join in!

Q: My class loves playing the games, but seems very reluctant to move on to the deeper discussion work and worksheets. How do I move the lesson on to get the round and activities moving so the circle has pace and covers the work I need it to?

A: The secret to this is in the planning. Have a wide repertoire of games to play and be familiar enough with them so that you know you can pull the learning you want out of the game. In the Bullying circle, for instance, the students can play games where people will definitely be left out or ' picked on'. Sixes or Racing Cars are good examples. You play the game. Ask the students how it felt, then move them into groups or pairs to discuss the issue, give them a sentence starter for the round and you're off. If they insist on more games, run them at the end. As the students mature and gain experience, it is good to try to give the control of games and even rounds and discussion to them so that they take the responsibility for the lesson. One kiss of death is when teachers start by having fun, playing some games, having a round and then get the worksheets out, following this pattern for every lesson. Alternative activities are important. If you need evidence of learning, then get the students to make posters, jot down thoughts or ideas for homework or create lists. They can create PowerPoint or role-play presentations to show what they have learned and understood.

Section Four

Examples of Circle Scripts

We have selected two circle scripts from each year group to show a broad range of how PSHE and Citizenship lessons can be run using Circle Time. These have all been tried and tested, so we would urge you to have a look and try them, even if you only begin by playing some games, highlighting the learning from them and having a scripted round. (A round is when each student in turn has the opportunity to speak. A scripted round is when the beginning of a sentence is provided and each student finishes it, such as 'My favourite food is …') Though the circle scripts presented in this section can be used as they stand, they can also be adapted to your own style to fit the group that you are teaching. In each script, we present some ideas for adapting the script to your own needs and some tips that will help you to run the circle more effectively. As you read the scripts, we suggest that you look at Section Five of the book on Games and access the Resources and References section at the back of the book, so that you are familiar with the relevant activities as you go along. Of course you can adapt scripts or mix and match games and activities as you like, but do beware of repeating the same games too often.

Bullying 1 (ages 11–12)

Bullying is a sensitive subject so the groundrules need to be reinforced at the beginning of each lesson. Keep alert to vulnerable students and possible difficulties in the group. Sometimes the games can expose covert bullying so with very difficult groups it would be a good idea to have the help of an extra adult such as an LSA.

Learning outcomes
Students:

▶   understand different forms of bullying
▶   support the unacceptability of bullying
▶   know some ways of dealing with bullying including school code of practice.

Beginning phase
Games
Play Name Chain to ensure that everyone knows everybody else's name.

Play Sixes with and without Guardian Angels. This game is played to introduce the idea of victims and bullies. Sometimes we can be deliberately picked on (when classmates gang up to get us 'killed' in the game) and sometimes the events that result in us being 'killed' are random. If this happens, it can be sensitively used as a discussion point after the game is played.

Play Racing Cars and point out how it feels to be left out.

Middle phase
Pairs
In pairs discuss what you think bullies do. The teacher and adult supporters can go round to help the discussions. Remember to include the breadth of bullying behaviour such as that which is physical, name calling, freezing out, gossiping and so on.

Open discussion

Each pair reports back to the whole group using the sentence 'We think that bullying can be ...' It is important to keep the group focused on the behaviours that are associated with bullies and not to get hooked into specific instances or any mention of specific people. The teacher can write up a list of bullying behaviours on the whiteboard or on a large sheet of paper in the centre of the circle.

Hold an open discussion about the difference between bullying behaviour and a bully.

G   *Game*

Play Silent Statements about bullying, using the sentence stem 'Cross the circle if ...' There are many statements that you can use to highlight bullying behaviours and ways of dealing with bullying. Some examples of statements you can use are listed below.

Cross the circle if ...

> ⇨   you think it is best to ignore bullying.
> ⇨   you think most bullies are or have been bullied themselves.
> ⇨   you think telling is the worst thing to do.
> ⇨   there are some parts of the school that you avoid.
> ⇨   you have ever helped someone who was being bullied.
> ⇨   you have ever bullied someone.
> ⇨   you have stood by while bullying took place.
> ⇨   you felt bullied by a teacher or a student.
> ⇨   you've said 'No' to bullying.

Pairs

Form new pairs in the circle. Give out situation cards, one to each pair (see pages 67–8 for some photocopiable examples). Get the students to read the card and think of ideas to help the person in this situation.

Open discussion

At the end of the paired discussion, feed back some ideas on how to deal with bullying. Make sure you draw attention to the school's code of practice for bullying.

Closing phase
Poem
Read the poem called 'The Bully' (inspired by *Poems for Circle Time and Literacy Hour* by Margaret Goldthorpe, reproduced on page 66). Students sit quietly and meditate on the poem. It helps to have quiet music playing.

Round
Have a round of 'Bullying is unacceptable because ...'

Personal reflection
If there is time, get students to make personal notes in notebooks or journals as a reflection on the lesson

Resources

- Speaking object
- Notebooks or journals and pens
- Situation cards on bullying
- 'The Bully' poem
- CD of quiet or gentle music.

The Bully

(By Tom Rambridge, aged 13)

Last year we all teased Ravi,

We stopped him playing games,

We nicked his stuff, we tripped him up.

We called him nasty names.

The teachers did not see us,

They did not seem to care,

We punched and spat on Ravi,

We laughed at his black hair.

Ravi, he got angry,

He sometimes went quite mad,

He shouted, cried and hit us,

He got in trouble bad.

Now Ravi's moved away from us,

He's gone to Weston Blue,

So now our gang is looking,

Perhaps we'll pick on you.

Situation Cards

1. A student in your class is always saying unpleasant things about your friend quietly when you are near. You try to ignore it but you know that it could easily be you next. When you ask your friend they say they're fine and the people are just stupid, but you know it's probably more than this.

2. Your friend's mum has just died, and some people in your group are making fun, saying rude and disrespectful things about her.

3. A student you don't know well always seems to be alone and unhappy. They often come to school late and don't have the correct uniform. They smell a bit sometimes. Everyone laughs at them and some people thump them or trip them up. You feel sorry but don't know what to do about it.

4. Your best friend from junior school has started to go round with a new crowd. They exclude you from their conversations and laugh together a lot. When you speak to your friend alone s/he's fine, but when they are with the new crowd they are nasty to you. They don't let you join in games at breaks.

5. The smokers in the school toilets have told everyone not to tell or they'll get 'done'. You avoid the toilets but now they're locked in lesson time so you have to go at breaks.

(Continued)

6. A student with additional needs is often teased. Yesterday you saw some older students take their bag and lunch. The student made it worse by laughing and when you asked if they were OK they said they were fine and that these people were their friends.

7. A student in your class thinks it's OK to make racist and sexist comments all the time. They think it's a laugh and make fun of you when you ask them to stop. Last time you asked them they started to say nasty things about you.

8. A new teacher seems to have it in for a student in your tutor set. Suddenly they are in lots of trouble, but you know it is not all one way. This teacher actually lied about what this student had done in the last lesson.

9. You have a new friend in school that has just arrived. You are looking out for them and settling them in but you notice that some of your pens, dinner money and small items are going missing. Yesterday you noticed the new friend was writing with your best pen.

10. You suspect a student in your group is having a lot of trouble at home. They are often away and sometimes have cuts and bruises.

Bullying 2 (ages 11–12)

Learning outcomes
Students:

▶ understand how it feels to be bullied
▶ consider causes of bullying
▶ understand their responsibility to deal with bullying.

Beginning phase
Games
Play Link Up. This game is played in silence.

Play Guess the Rule. Play one round where the 'detectives' try to fathom out the rule that the group is working to.

Open discussion
Discuss how people feel when they are 'in the know' and how others feel when they are excluded. Ask the class to provide examples of including and excluding others, such as leaving people out of conversations or deciding with a small group of friends what is 'cool' and making others feel uncomfortable because they aren't 'cool'.

Game
Play Fruit Salad using Simpsons characters such as Bart, Lisa, Millhouse and so on. The teacher links ideas about the various types of bullying and reminds the group about the last lesson.

Middle phase
Stimulus for discussion
Provide some stimulus material around bullying. You can use a story, a news item, or a video clip from *Grange Hill* and so on. You need to select something that is topical and powerful so that it engenders an emotional response from the students.

Pairs
In pairs have a discussion about the reasons for bullying, during which the teacher circulates to ensure responses are broad, thought out and varied.

Round
Have a round where each pair agrees what they will say to finish the sentence 'We think bullies bully others because ...'

Agony Aunt letters
Give pairs Agony Aunt letters (see page 71 for a photocopiable example) and ask them to decide what they think is going on and what advice they would give to the person who wrote the letter. A pair then joins another pair to make four and share their ideas again to see if they learn anything new. (Pair, square, share.)

Open discussion
Take feedback in the whole group on reasons for bullying and possible actions. It is sometimes good to take notes on flip chart paper in the centre of the circle.

Discuss in the whole group and come to agreement about ways of dealing with bullying. There is no one solution and students need to try several. Should everyone take it on themselves not to bully and to support others?

Personal reflection
The personal reflection for this lesson can take different forms. Either encourage students to write a few notes in their notebooks on their personal responsibility to deal with bullying, or ask students to write a response to one of the situations that has been discussed during the lesson.

Closing phase

Game
Play No Laughing Matter!

Resources

- Speaking object
- Notebooks and pens
- Video clip, story or stimulus for discussion in middle phase
- Agony Aunt Letters.

Agony Aunt Letter

Dear Agony Aunt,

Every day on my way to school a group of
kids shout names at me and sometimes take
my bag and empty it in the street.

Can you help me?

Yours Sincerely,

Charlie Dobbes

Healthy living — Sleep (ages 12—13)

This lesson plan can be used as an introduction to the need for sufficient sleep. A follow-up homework exercise could be to keep a sleep diary. If you decide to extend the lesson to look at sleep patterns over the next week, you will need to have prepared a sleep diary pro-forma for students to use and we suggest that you keep your own sleep diary to use as an example. Further resources are available from the Wired For Health website (see the section on 'Useful websites' at the end of the book).

Learning outcomes
Students:

▶ know the amount of sleep recommended for their age
▶ know the consequences of insufficient sleep
▶ consider their own sleep needs and sleep patterns.

Beginning phase
Ⓖ *Games*

Play Silent Statements using the sentence stem 'Cross the circle if you ...' Some examples of statements you can use are listed below.

Cross the circle if you . . .

> ⇨ went to bed after 11p.m.
> ⇨ had breakfast this morning.
> ⇨ had eight or more hours of sleep last night.
> ⇨ often can't sleep.
> ⇨ sleep very well.
> ⇨ find it hard to get up most mornings.

Play Wink Sleep.

Middle phase
Pairs

Pairs discuss times when it is easy and difficult to get to sleep.

Round

Follow the paired discussion with a round where each individual completes the sentence 'I find that I sleep best when ...' If the round takes a short time, it can be extended by a second round of 'When I can't sleep I ...' or 'I find it hard to get to bed early when ...'

Open discussion

After the round, have a brief open discussion to bring together the issues raised in the round(s). The teacher can make some summary remarks if it is appropriate.

Stimulus for discussion

Make up two different sleep diaries for two fictitious students (see page 75 for a photocopiable example). One sleeps well and one hardly sleeps at all. Draw out the learning from the two diaries. Hold a discussion about the benefits of enough sleep for children, adolescents, adults, stressed people, the unfit or ill.

Give students some facts about sleep such as those found on the Stanford University website (www.stanford.edu):

Sleep facts

1. Adolescents need nine to nine and a half hours of sleep a night.
2. Children need ten hours.
3. Adults need eight and a quarter hours.
4. Teenagers rarely get enough sleep due to early school start time and an inability to fall asleep until late at night, or have work, social life and homework commitments.
5. Parents may need to adjust their child's schedule to allow more sleep.
6. Most teens are chronically sleep deprived and try to 'catch up' on their sleep by sleeping in at the weekend.
7. Ultimately they should go to bed and wake up at the same time everyday.

Open discussion

Ask for a volunteer who has a problem with sleep or create a fictitious student. The group gives hints or advice to help.

Personal reflection

If there is time, ask students to reflect individually on how much sleep they get each night and in a week. Set a personal target to ensure that they get enough sleep. Each student writes her own target in a notebook or journal and shares it with her partner.

Closing phase
Relaxation

End with group relaxation either seated or lying down using soft music, dim lights, drawn curtains, deep breathing and muscle relaxation.

Game

An alternative ending is to play silent Bottle Swap or silent Where's the Object?

Resources

- Speaking object
- Notebook or journal and pens
- Sleep diaries for the two fictitious students
- CD of quiet music.

Sleep diaries

Diary 1

Day	Monday	Tuesday	Wednesday	Thursday	Friday
Time to bed	9 p.m.				
Hours' sleep	8				
Quality	Good				

Diary 2

Day	Monday	Tuesday	Wednesday	Thursday	Friday
Time to bed	12 a.m.				
Hours' sleep	5				
Quality	Poor. Went to toilet 2 a.m.				

Healthy living: body images and peer pressure (ages 12-13)

This lesson can be extended by giving homework to compliment at least five people on their appearance this week and to note down any compliments paid to you. Draw attention to giving and receiving compliments to encourage people to feel positive about their image no matter whether it is an 'in' image or not.

Learning outcomes
Students:

▶ consider groups of people in school who have particular images
▶ understand the effect of peer pressure on image
▶ feel positive about personal image.

Beginning phase
(G) *Game*
Play Silent Statements to recap the last lesson and introduce the current lesson. Use the sentence stem 'Cross the circle if you ...' Some examples of statements you can use are listed below.

Cross the circle if you ...

> ⇨ did the sleep diary homework.
> ⇨ managed to get eight hours' or more sleep most nights.
> ⇨ got less that eight hours' sleep at the weekend.
> ⇨ discuss clothes with your friends.
> ⇨ enjoy shopping for clothes.
> ⇨ think it matters what you wear.
> ⇨ take extra care over non-uniform days.
> ⇨ feel you belong to a particular group.

Middle phase
This week we're looking at our bodies again. This time we are considering our appearance.

Pairs
In pairs discuss what you wear on non-uniform days.

76

Round

Have a round where each person completes the sentence 'On non-uniform days I wear …'

Pairs

In pairs discuss what advice you would give a new student about what to wear on non-uniform days.

Open discussion

Take feedback from the pairs on the advice they would give to a new student. In the whole group, discuss non-uniform days and the sort of clothes people wear. How do they choose what to wear?

Move the discussion on to the school uniform. What do students like about the school uniform? What don't they like? Remember to take the discussion wider than the actual uniform to include the accessories such as hats and school bags.

Are clothes important? What do they say about us? Does it matter if we are all different? How do you know or decide what's 'cool'? Who says which backpacks, coats, bags are the ones that we should choose?

Pairs

In pairs jot down ten uniform tips for a new student aged 12 or 13 who is joining the school.

Small groups

Move the pairs into groups of four and ask them to agree between them the ten most important uniform tips. When the fours have agreed their ten tips, join groups of four together to make groups of eight. Once again the group of eight has to agree the ten most important tips for the group.

Open discussion

Take feedback in the whole group from the three or four groups of eight. Draw out the learning about the images we want to portray and the people or groups that put pressure on us to look a certain way. This part will only be used if the non-uniform discussion is short or inappropriate. Otherwise it could be adapted to use in another circle on image or self-esteem.

Draw the middle phase to a close by getting the group to nominate people in the class who are their own people, that is, they never follow the crowd and have their own style. Take time to appreciate the qualities that enable individuals to be themselves and to dress in a way that represents them.

Closing phase
Game

Play Guess the Rule, making the rule in relation to clothing or appearance.

Personal reflection

Close with a brief personal reflection on the judgements we make from appearance and the kind of image we want to portray by our own appearance.

Resources

- Speaking object
- Notebooks and pens.

How to say 'No' and remain friends (ages 13-14)

The subject of maintaining friendship while assertively resisting pressure to do things you don't want to do is an ever-present reality for students aged 13 and 14. This can be a sensitive issue, so if you are unfamiliar with the group, ask the tutor about any difficulties or vulnerable students to look out for. It might be helpful to have a back-up plan such as access to the school counsellor so that you can follow up any issues that arise during the discussion.

Learning outcomes
Students:

▶ consider the pressure that people can put us under
▶ are able to say 'No' assertively
▶ resist pressure from others to behave in a way which would make them feel uncomfortable.

Beginning phase
Games

Play Racing Cars, Bouncing Ball or Sixes. Any of these games can be played so that people are excluded and experience the feelings associated with being left out.

Play Name Chain or Aliens. Either of these games provides an experience of being chosen and not being chosen.

Play Silent Statements. This lesson, play a variation of the Silent Statements game using the sentence stem 'You can cross the bridge if you ...' Some examples of statements you can use are listed below.

You can cross the bridge if you ...

> ⇨ are wearing a ring.
> ⇨ own a Gap or Nike top.
> ⇨ had a shower this morning.
> ⇨ like Goths (or a group in your school).
> ⇨ belong to a gang.
> ⇨ like garage music.
> ⇨ have any Nike clothes.
> ⇨ have designer trainers on.

Middle phase

The opening games have all been about belonging and not belonging; being part of and being left out.

Pairs

Pairs discuss 'Being part of a group or gang involves ...' then feedback in a round.

The next part of the lesson examines whether we always want to be part of a group and whether we are willing to do the things or wear the clothes that allow us entry into the group. Sometimes we have to be able to withstand pressure from our peers without offending our friends or appearing to be a 'nerd' or 'loser'.

Open discussion

Hold a discussion in the whole group using questions such as: What is a 'gang' or 'group'? Why do people belong to them? Which groups are represented in this school? What do they look like?

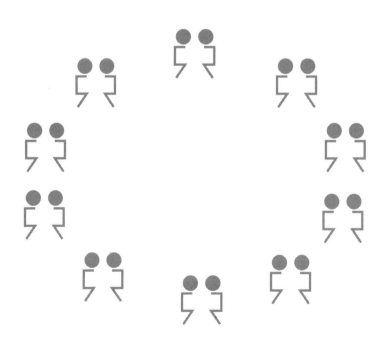

Practise saying 'No'

In this activity get the class to form two circles. This is best done by getting every second person in the circle to lift their chair, turn it round and place it to face the person who was sitting to their right. The students are now sat in two circles, with an inner circle facing out and an outer circle facing in. The pairs face each other. The person in the outer circle tries to persuade the person in the inner circle to do something such as smoke, try drugs, drink alcohol, lie, bully, skive a lesson and so on. The person in the inner circle has to find ways of saying 'No, I don't want to' without being offensive. At the end of each one- or two-minute discussion, the people in the inner circle stay still and those in the outer circle move one space clockwise so that they have a new partner for the next discussion. Students can decide whether to stick with the same topic or to change it. Make sure that after two or three discussions, you swap round so that the people in the outer circle say 'No' and those in the inner circle do the persuading. Some groups may find this difficult. You could skip it and go on to using the situation cards next.

Situation cards

If time allows, move the discussion on to situations when this kind of thing happens in real life (see page 82 for some photocopiable situation cards). It is a good idea to use situation cards in pairs. The pair is to give advice on how to say 'No' to a student who finds themselves in the situation on the card.

Open discussion

The students put the chairs back into one big circle. In the whole group, take feedback to find out how students felt when they were put under pressure to do something that they didn't want to do. How did they say 'No'? What tone of voice did they use? Did they give excuses? What does an assertive 'No' sound like and look like?

Closing phase
Round

Finish off the situation cards activity by having a round. Use the sentence stem 'I said yes when I really wanted to say no when ...' or 'I'm pleased that I said no when ...'

Resources

- Speaking object
- Situation cards on how to say 'No'.

Situations Cards

1. A friend tries to get you to smoke a cigarette and you don't want to.

2. Someone wants you to drink alcohol at a party. You are under age and you don't want to drink alcohol until you are older.

3. There is a party going on and your friend wants you to go. Your parents won't let you, so the friend urges you to lie to your parents so you can stay out late.

4. Your partner wants to go further sexually than you are happy to.

5. Someone wants to borrow your trainers or kit.

6. Someone invites you round and you don't want to go.

Improving the school (ages 13–14)

This Circle Time is about working in a group and being able to compromise in order for a group to reach consensus. The format can be used and adapted for any issue that calls for student consultation. It is really important to ensure that all suggestions are encouraged and considered, even if they are wildly impossible or expensive. You will find that you do not have to censor any contribution because as the lesson progresses, the group will weed out the impossible ideas and produce a rational decision. The lesson can be extended into a homework assignment which asks groups of students to create detailed presentations (using either PowerPoint or other visual aids) to support their idea. At the next lesson, the presentations are viewed and then the class decides which idea to take forward to the school council.

Learning outcomes
Students:

▶ participate in a group activity
▶ negotiate and make decisions as part of a group
▶ make compromises to reach consensus
▶ know about school issues on which they can have an impact.

Beginning phase
Ⓖ *Games*
Play Link Up

Play Bing, Bang, Boing!

Emphasise the importance of co-operation and teamwork when playing these games.

Open discussion
Take feedback from the group about working together. Draw out the things that make it easy or difficult to work together. What things sabotage working together and how do these make us feel? Highlight the need to work together in order to make a good decision that represents everyone's views for the school council.

Middle phase
Small groups
In groups of three, students use a large piece of paper to write down all the improvements they would like to see in the school. Start by allowing them to think of any improvement they would like to see, no matter how impractical or expensive it might be.

In the group, select and agree the top five improvements which are sensible, practical and affordable. Each group of three joins another three to make a six. Share the improvements each group has talked about and in the six agree on a top priority.

Open discussion
Take feedback from the groups of six on their agreed priorities for making the school a better place to be. Make a list of the suggested improvements on a large piece of paper in the middle of the circle.

Small group presentations
Each group of six prepares a one-minute presentation on their proposal with arguments as to why their idea is best.

Open discussion
The presentations are heard and the whole group discusses the different ideas and then votes to find the majority view. The whole group discusses an action plan for taking the idea to the school council.

Closing phase
Pairs
In pairs discuss how your group reached agreement on the top priority. How well did it work? How did you feel about the decision that was reached?

Open discussion
Take feedback in the group about things that stop groups reaching decisions. What methods of decision making were used in the class? Did they all work equally well? How will groups reach a joint decision in future?

Round

Have a round of 'Next time I work in a group, I will help the group by ...' Everyone writes their target in their notebook or journal.

Resources

- Speaking object
- Notebooks and pens
- Flip chart paper and pens.

Starting exam courses (ages 14–15)

The students have spent their lower school years as a coherent group of learners. They have been taught as a group for many subjects and as they move into the upper school and select subjects to study for public examinations they may find themselves in new groups with students they have hardly met before. This lesson can be used as part of the PSHE course or in tutorial time to draw attention to the need for students to make relationships in their new subject groups. It also presents an opportunity for students to consider the opportunities and challenges of the next two years as they prepare for their first set of public examinations.

If this lesson is done with a new group of students who don't know one another, it is important to make sure that there are no put-downs or negative naming so that you create an emotionally safe environment in which to look at the issues. Either establish groundrules if the group is new, or remind them of the groundrules at the start. Look at how raise a problem with a teacher and reflect on taking action to resolve problems. Playing name games such as All About You will also help the group's cohesion and safety.

Learning outcomes
Students:

▶ review the transfer from lower school to upper school as they start their examination courses
▶ have a sense of purpose about this stage of their lives
▶ want to get the best out the next two years of exam preparation
▶ consider the challenges of working in a new group.

Beginning phase
Game
Play Sixes. This is played to show people being left out and to highlight the choices that the group makes about who to isolate.

Open discussion

Discuss how it felt to be out of the game early. Is it always chance that causes us to be left out or is there some choice?

Game

Play Name Chain. This game is played to mix everyone up and to ensure that people know each other's names and have the chance to find out something about them (this could lead into a discussion about where and who to sit with in a new group).

Middle phase

Pairs

Discuss the subjects you have chosen to study for public exams with your partner and the changes that this stage in your life brings.

Round

For the round use the sentence stem 'One change I really like this year is …'

Depending on the response to the first round, you could have a second one using the sentence stem 'One thing that bothers me about this year is …'

Open discussion

Pick up on the information and feelings shared. Draw out any commonly held views such as expectations, opportunities, concerns, fears or goals. If there are a lot of concerns in the group, discuss the changes they have made since the first year of secondary school. Focusing on the positive developments they have already made helps the students to think about the possibility of success in the future.

Small groups

Make up small groups by numbering round the circle from one to five then repeating one to five and so on. All the people numbered one work together, all the twos and so on. There should be approximately five groups of six students in a class of thirty. Give each group a sheet of flip chart paper and large pens. Ask them to divide the paper in half so that they can make two lists. The first list is things that make a lesson bad. The second list is what makes a lesson interesting. Each group then discusses the advice they would give to a teacher who has a new exam group. How would they advise the teacher to get the best out of the group and ensure that they work well together?

Open discussion

Share each group's advice. Discuss the role that the teacher plays and the responsibility of individual students in making sure they get the best out of the next two years.

Closing phase
Personal reflection

Each student considers two goals. They set themselves one goal which is short term to help them cope with the new timetable and year group. The second goal is longer term and involves looking forward to the results at the end of the examination period and writing down the outcome they hope for. Record both goals in the student planner or in their notebooks.

Resources

- Speaking object (by the time students reach the age of 15, some staff no longer want to use a speaking object. The teacher or group facilitator will have to decide whether it is still needed)
- Notebooks and pens
- Flip chart paper and pens.

Preparing for work experience (ages 14–15)

This is the lesson the week before the students go off on work experience so it assumes that most or all of the students already know where they are going for their placements. The lesson plan provides a wealth of material which can be used to focus on practical preparation for work experience or health and safety issues. We have given you resources and activities for both so you will need to choose and adapt the script to meet your needs. There is also the possibility of inviting visitors to the circle in the form of older students who can share their experiences and act as consultants to the group or a Connexions or Careers adviser. The lesson plan can be adapted by removing the paired work after the Silent Statements game and omitting the I Packed My Bag game. The time is used for getting the pairs to prepare questions for the visitor(s) after the quiz and then asking the questions in the open discussion. An extension activity that can be used for homework is to ask students to prepare a list of 'Top Ten Tips for Work Experience' that can be given to the next year's students when they are preparing for work experience.

Learning outcomes
Students:

▶ explore feelings about work experience
▶ understand the need to be thoroughly prepared for work experience
▶ know what to prepare
▶ make an action plan that facilitates their enjoyment of work experience.

Beginning phase

Game
Play Line Up! Use a continuum from 'Very confident' to 'Really worried' about next week's work experience.

Pairs

When students have stood on the line, ask them to discuss with the nearest person to them the reasons for choosing their position on the continuum line.

Game

Play Silent Statements using the sentence stem 'Cross the circle if you ...' Some example of statements you can use are listed below.

Cross the circle if you ...

⇨   have the work placement you wanted.
⇨   know how to get to your work placement.
⇨   have got your clothes sorted.
⇨   are looking forward to work experience.
⇨   have your log book.
⇨   feel nervous.
⇨   have filled in the introductory sections of your log book.

Middle phase

Pairs

Put the group into pairs in the circle and ask them to discuss the plans they have made for work experience. This discussion provides the information for the next game.

Game

Play I Packed My Bag using the sentence stem 'I packed my bag for work experience and in it I put ...' The idea of this game is to gather together as many different aspects of work experience as possible and to stimulate thinking and planning for the work experience week.

Questionnaire

Give out the work experience questionnaire on pages 93–4 for students to fill in individually.

Pairs

Put the class into pairs and ask them to jot down advice that they would give to another pair about preparing for work experience.

Small groups

Join two pairs together to give advice to one another.

Open discussion

As a whole group have an open discussion which begins with students highlighting things that they may encounter using the question 'What happens if ...?' Problems and solutions are fed back and opened up to the whole group in the circle for discussion of solutions.

Closing phase

Play Line Up! by asking the students to stand on continuum lines from 'Completely prepared' to 'Completely unprepared'. Then revisit the continuum from the beginning of the lesson that went from 'Very confident' to 'Really worried' and ask the students to reflect on whether they feel more confident about work experience than they did at the beginning of the lesson.

Round

Have a round using the sentence stem 'I'm looking forward to ... and I still need to ...'

Resources

- Speaking object (optional at this age and stage)
- Work experience questionnaire copied for each student
- Pens for filling in the questionnaire.

Work experience questionnaire

1. On my first day I'm going to wear . . . .
   . . . .

2. I'm travelling to my placement by . . . .
   . . . .

3. I have to be at work by . . . .
   . . . .

4. I have to set my alarm for . . . .
   . . . .

5. The person in charge of me is called . . . .
   . . . .

6. For lunch I will . . . .
   . . . .

7. My hours are . . . .
   . . . .

8. I'm hoping to . . . .
   . . . .

9. My supervisor is called . . . .
   . . . .

10. I rang my work placement on . . . .
    . . . .

11. My school contact is . . . .
    . . . .

(Continued)

12.   The emergency telephone number is . . . .

. . . .

13.   On my work experience I will be expected to . . . .

. . . .

14.   My log book has to be finished by . . . .

. . . .

15.   The point of work experience is . . . .

. . . .

1.   Sexual harassment means . . . .

. . . .

2.   If I am asked to carry very heavy, dirty
objects I will . . . .

. . . .

3.   If a fellow worker pressurises me to
do something I don't want to do I will . . . .

. . . .

4.   Equal opportunities means . . . .

. . . .

5.   If I don't get a lunch break I will . . . .

. . . .

6.   If I am not learning anything I will . . . .

. . . .

Sexual orientation (ages 15–16)

Sexual orientation is a controversial and sensitive subject for discussion. It is really important that you plan carefully and that you have some flexibility in your lesson plan to allow for the mood of the group. You may need to remind students of the groundrules so that there is no homophobic language or put-downs. It is worth thinking about TV soaps, media stories and celebrities that could support the lesson and that you highlight any stereotypes that emerge when you are playing games or doing rounds. You may also want to visit the web-site www. wiredfor health.gov.uk for definitions and useful information. The script is particularly long because some activities will be more successful than others in any particular group. We have given you a range of alternatives so that you can choose the ones that work best for you.

An extension activity is to ask the students to think about the issues raised in the lesson and to look out for a storyline in a film, book, magazine or TV programme that touches on these issues to bring to the next lesson.

Learning outcomes
Students:

▸ know correct terminology for different types of sexual orientation
▸ examine personal assumptions about people who have a different sexual orientation from themselves
▸ become aware of sexual stereotypes.

Beginning phase
Explain that students can work in friendship groups today. At the very start of the lesson, ask the students to move so that they are sat next to people with whom they can work comfortably. As the facilitator of the circle, you need to watch out for any isolated or vulnerable students who may have been left out of friendship groups and you will need to attach them to a group without fuss.

Game

Play Alliterative Adjectives (page 117). Students think of a positive adjective that starts with the same letter as their first name such as 'mountaineering Marilyn'. This is an opportunity to diffuse tension with humour. It works especially well if the adverbs chosen are light-hearted such as 'Super, slinky Sue'. Make sure that you carefully monitor any disrespectful or abusive adverbs by using the groundrules.

Play Racing Pictionary. The list of words for the game should include relevant subjects such as a French man, a gay celebrity, a religious figure, a pop star.

Open discussion

After the games, pull out the stereotypes that have been drawn and discuss how readily they are understood.

Game

Play a version of Silent Statements that asks students to give their view without moving from one place to another in the circle. The lack of movement means that they remain in the friendship groups that they began in at the start of the lesson.

Statements might include:

> ⇨   Put your hands on your head if you think that it's wrong to be gay.
> ⇨   Cross your legs if you think that gay people should not be parents.
> ⇨   Stand up if you think that all lesbians look butch.
> ⇨   Put your hand up if you think gay men are camp.
> ⇨   Cross your arms if you think that gays should not work with children.
> ⇨   Thumbs up if you think gays are OK.

Middle phase

Pairs

Put the students into friendship pairs (there may be some groups of three if the numbers are not even or if some students are in danger of being left out). Give out large sheets of paper and flip chart pens and ask the students to make a list of terms that are used to describe people and their sexuality such as 'straight', 'gay' and so on. The

96

terms can include street names, slang terms, derogatory terms and correct terms. The students check that they know what the terms mean in their groups and then highlight the terms that are acceptable to use when writing formally about sexual orientation.

Open discussion
Take feedback on the acceptable terms that the different pairs know. Make a central list of the acceptable terms and discuss the definitions. This is the teacher's opportunity to make sure that the students know the correct terms and their definitions such as bisexual, lesbian, homosexual, heterosexual, transsexual, and so on. A photocopiable list of definitions has been provided on page 98.

Small groups
Put the students into friendship groups of five or six. The group forms its own small circle and makes a list of as many celebrities as they can think of who are not heterosexual. See if they can think of a celebrity for each of the types of sexual orientation. Discuss whether these people are seen positively or negatively and why.

Open discussion
Take feedback on the responses that people have to different sexual orientations and draw out the sexual stereotypes that we hold. There may be an opportunity to point out that sexuality is a private matter and we often do not know someone's sexual orientation and that we may be making assumptions based on prejudice rather than knowledge.

Closing phase
Round
Have a round in the group using the sentence stem 'One thing we have learned today is ...' or 'One thing I was surprised by today was ...'

Resources

- Speaking object (optional at this age and stage)
- Prepared definitions of different types of sexual orientation
- Pens and large sheets of paper.

Definitions of sexual orientation types

Homosexual	–	Someone who is attracted to someone of the same sex.

Celibate	–	Someone who chooses not to be sexually active.

Bisexual	–	Someone who is attracted to both sexes.

Transsexual	–	Someone who changes from one gender to another.

Heterosexual	–	Someone who is attracted to someone of the opposite sex.

These definitions came from a Year 11 PHSE group.

Where will I be in five years' time? (ages 15–16)

This is a lesson that allows students to think about what they aspire to and the steps they need to take to achieve their goals. If you have time in the session, or want to set a homework, an extension activity involves students writing a letter to themselves about their ambitions and hopes as if the school will post the letters to them in five years' time. Or they could write a personal reflection to record some of their thoughts and feelings.

Learning outcomes
Students:

▶ consider aspirations and ambitions for the next five years
▶ consider the steps needed to realise life goals
▶ think positively about their ability to make a difference in their own lives.

Beginning phase

Game
Play Mexican Wave. This game is played by getting the students to call out something that they really like as their arms go up. The wave then involves a succession of body movements and a list of things that the people in the group enjoy or like. You can extend the game by reversing the direction of the wave and changing the theme to something they want to do, or something they would really like to have.

Round
Introduce the round by talking about the theme of the lesson. They are going to consider their futures and what they would like to do in the next few years and what they want to have achieved by the time they are 21. Use the sentence stem 'In five years' time I hope to be ...'

The first round can be followed by a second using the sentence stem 'In ten years time I hope to be ...'

Middle phase
Personal reflection

Give each person a piece of paper, or ask them to use their notebooks. On a double page, ask the students to draw a timeline for the next ten years. They need to mark on it the things they would like to have done such as getting at least six high grades in the public examinations, finding a long-term girlfriend or boyfriend, going to college, visiting a foreign country, going on holiday without their family and so on. The timeline logs academic, personal and social ambitions and aspirations at the appropriate age. The students then have to fill in the steps that they need to take in order to achieve their aims.

Pairs

Put the students into pairs, or ask them to choose a partner they feel comfortable working with. The pair share their timelines and ask each other questions about how they are going to reach their goals. They may need to think about money, loans, part-time jobs, qualifications and so on.

Ask them to consider key questions:

> ⇨ What is important in your future plans?
> ⇨ What is likely to help you succeed?
> ⇨ What might stop you achieving your goals?
> ⇨ How can we overcome the obstacles to success?

Closing phase
Open discussion

In the whole group ask group members to share some of their ambitions and aspirations. Discuss what is needed to ensure that people get a good chance of a secure future. Ask if anyone would share with the whole group a goal that he thinks might be difficult to achieve. Use the circle to talk about the situation with him. The group can problem solve any obstacles to achieving the goal.

Round

Finish with a closing round using the sentence stem 'The first step I need to take towards my future is ...'

Resources

- Speaking object (optional at this age and stage)
- A4 paper
- Pens
- Notebooks.

Are humans animals? (ages 16-17)

This lesson plan is suitable for any students of 16 or 17 who are studying General Studies. It demonstrates how philosophical discussion can work within a circle. The topic is open-ended and therefore very fluid. The script for this lesson is deliberately loose to allow students to explore difficult issues step by step and at their own pace. The pictures and music will reflect your choice as teacher and circle facilitator. You may also want some different definitions of 'humanity' or 'animals' to give the group if they find the concepts hard to discuss at first.

Learning outcomes
Students:
▶ develop a group definition of 'human' and 'animal'
▶ consider whether humans have a special place that is different from animals
▶ think about personal views on moral and ethical issues to do with animals.

Beginning phase
Favourite pictures
Make a collection of pictures of different animals. Put four or five pictures out on the floor and ask students to move towards the picture that they like best. Once they have chosen their favourite picture, they turn to a neighbour and say what they like about it and why it is better than the other pictures from their point of view. The pictures can be changed and the activity repeated if the discussion is good.

Round
Have a round to introduce the theme of the lesson. In the round, use the sentence stem 'If I was an animal I'd be a ... because ...'

Middle phase

Pairs
In pairs ask the students to talk about the difference between animals and humans. Are there any ways in which humans are different or special?

Open discussion

Take feedback from the pairs in the whole group and come to a consensual understanding of animals, humans and any differences between the two.

Pairs

Give out large sheets of paper and pens to pairs of students and ask them to make two lists. One list is the characteristics of humans and the other, the characteristics of animals.

Small groups

A pair joins with another pair to compare their lists. Each pair explains their sheet to the other. They clarify the information and answer questions about their lists.

Open discussion

The groups of four feed back to the whole group and in an open discussion, the teacher draws out the moral, aesthetic, spiritual and emotional aspects of being human. As the information is brought together, come to an agreed definition of 'human' and 'animal' in the whole group.

Game

Play Line Up! One end of the line is 'Agree' and the other end, 'Disagree'. Ask students to stand on the line in relation to the following statements. Once they have chosen their place on the line, ask them to discuss the issue briefly with the people around them.

Issues for Line Up

⇨ Animal experimentation is OK for cosmetics and drugs.
⇨ Vegetarianism is better than eating meat.
⇨ Hunting of animals should be freely allowed in this country.
⇨ Fishing should be illegal.
⇨ Genetic engineering in animals should be supported by government funding.

Open discussion

If the students have been discussing freely during the Line Up! game, you can move towards a philosophical debate on man's place in the world in relation to the animal kingdom. This debate can be informed by different world views such as a Christian, Hindu, Humanist and so on.

Alternatively, the open discussion may centre on cruelty to animals or the value of life.

Closing phase
Personal reflection
Put on some calm music and ask the students to reflect on their position in relation to animals and to consider whether humans have a special place in the world that is different from animals. Has their view changed as a result of the discussion in this lesson? Students can write a personal reflection in their notebooks.

Resources

- Speaking object (optional at this age and stage)
- Pictures or postcards of animals
- Notebooks and pens
- Music for the personal reflection
- Definitions of human and animal from a dictionary.

The Survival game: why have rules? (ages 16–17)

This is a lesson plan that can be used for PSHE, Citizenship or for an exam course in General Studies. It encourages analytical thinking about rules and roles in groups and uses the groups' feedback to highlight the political processes involved. It might be helpful to look for a TV programme or media story such as 'Lost' to stimulate discussion and to highlight the roles that people play, the rules that emerge and the value of everyone's contribution to a group situation.

Learning outcomes
Students:

▶ understand the roles people play in groups and in daily life
▶ consider the value of rules in society
▶ consider how rules are generated and implemented.

Beginning phase

Ⓖ *Game*
Play Line Up! The class line up according to their birthdays (day and month, not year) in silence.

Once the line is formed, the teacher can number the students 'one, two, three, four, five' repeated down the line so that all the number ones form a group, the twos form a second group and so on. This should give five groups of five or six students in a class of 25 to 30 students.

Middle phase
Survival simulation
Each group is going to work out how their team will manage in a given situation. They are prisoners in a camp and they are trying to survive. The following bullet points define the conditions in the camp and they cannot be changed. The students have to work with the conditions they are given in order to survive. It is helpful to write the conditions on an overhead projector (OHP) or on the board as a reminder to the students.

▶ There is no escape.

▶ They have four weeks' worth of food; a hammer and nails; three two-man tents; packets of seeds and two goats.

▶ There is a stream and a ruined building.

Timed tasks

Each team has five minutes to agree on each task below:

1. Sleeping arrangements
2. Daily tasks
3. Allocation of jobs.

Open discussion

At the end of the five minutes each team feeds back to the whole group the decisions they have made about the three tasks. They are also asked to report on how they reached a decision. Talk about different kinds of decision making and the level of commitment people have to the final decision in relation to the way the decision is made.

Small groups

The students go back into their small groups and discuss the following topics:

⇨ Do you as a group want or need a leader?

⇨ If you have a leader, how do you select him or her?

⇨ Do you need rules in order to survive?

⇨ If you have rules, what would they be?

⇨ What will you do if someone disobeys the rules?

Role play

The teams of five or six students work with any rules they have made and their understanding of leadership to role play one or more of the scenarios given below. It might be helpful to have each scenario written on a piece of card so that one can be given out to each group and swapped round if there is time.

1. Somebody has eaten all the food and there are no reserves left.
2. One person refuses to do their allocated duties.
3. One person becomes too ill to work and needs constant nursing.
4. One person dies.
5. A small splinter group forms.

Open discussion

After each role play, the teams come back to the circle to share their experiences. It is good to provide a focus for the discussions and you can choose which focus to use as you watch the role plays unfold and decide which would be the most appropriate. Possible subjects for discussion might be:

▶ Do rules help in getting tasks done?
▶ What roles do people play in a team situation?
▶ How helpful are the different roles?

Closing phase
Personal reflection

Encourage students to reflect on the different roles they took in the team and how well they helped the team to perform the various tasks. (It might help to jot different roles on the board such as: leaders; followers; rebels; blockers; jokers; and so on.) You can provide these roles out of the discussion that has already taken place, or ask the students to provide them.

Invite the students to reflect on the role(s) they played today in this lesson and on roles they play in other groups.

Resources

- Speaking object (optional at this age and stage)
- Notebooks and pens
- Role-play scenario cards (optional).

The Twenty Pound Note game (ages 17–18)

This lesson is suitable for older students in a PSHE or Citizenship lesson or as part of a General Studies course. The script can also be adapted to introduce an ethics course as it introduces the ideas of ethics, morality and what motivates us to behave in a 'good' way. It is helpful to prepare for the lesson by looking for issues that are currently in the news and apply them to the discussion.

Learning outcomes
Students:
▶ consider personal ethics
▶ understand how we make moral choices.

Beginning phase
Ⓖ *Game*

Play Silent Statements. In this game, use the statements about moral issues that are provided with the script or make up your own ethical or moral situations to suit the group. The game begins with the sentence stem 'Cross the circle if you ...'

⇨ think all lies are wrong.
⇨ think 'white' lies are OK.
⇨ have ever told a lie.
⇨ have kept something you found.
⇨ have ever broken something and not owned up.
⇨ have ever let someone else take the blame for something you did.
⇨ have ever borrowed something and not returned it.

Ⓖ *Game*

Play I Packed My Bag with the sentence stem 'If I had twenty pounds, I would buy ...'

Middle phase
Tell the group that you have hidden a twenty pound note in the room. (It is up to you if you want to actually do this!) Each person in the room will need to make a decision about what they would do if they found it.

108

Pairs

Put the students into pairs and ask them to discuss what their options are if they find the £20.

Open discussion

Take feedback from the pairs in the whole group on what the students would do if they found the £20. Expect a range of views which could include return it to you, hand it to the office, keep it, spend it, give it to charity and so on.

Small groups

Put the pairs together to make groups of four. Ask the students to discuss in their group what they would do if they found the £20 and to explain to each other what their motive would be.

Hot seat

Place a chair in the middle of the circle and ask for a volunteer to take the seat and explain what he would do with the money and why. Invite the students in the rest of the group to question the person in the middle to check out what his motive is and to explain it. The students in the circle can take on different roles such as a parent, the police, the head teacher, a friend and so on when they ask the questions.

The hot-seating activity can be repeated choosing different students who hold different viewpoints. It is important that you are open to a range of different motivations such as 'It feels good to do the right thing'; 'I'd be embarrassed if I was caught keeping it'; 'I'd keep it'; 'I need it more than you do'; 'I'd return it because it belongs to you' and so on.

Small groups

Return to groups to discuss which of the moral choices have been affected by family values, rules, religious beliefs or selfish motives. The debate may move to why we find it difficult to live according to our beliefs.

If there is time, the discussion can be extended by adding in ideas such as:

⇨ What if you were a Utilitarian and wanted the best outcome for the greatest number?

⇨ What would a Christian do?

⇨ Which is more important, goodness or social conformity?

⇨ What matters most, intent or outcome?

Closing phase
Personal reflection

Bring the students back to the circle and have a moment of personal reflection. If they found the twenty pound note, what would they really do? Is their decision different from the one they had at the beginning of the lesson? On what basis would they make their decision now? The reflections can be written in a planner or student notebook or they can be spoken about in the group.

Resources

- Speaking object (optional at this age and stage)
- Twenty pound note (optional)
- Planners or notebooks
- Pens.

Taking risks (ages 17–18)

This is a PSHE lesson that allows older and more independent students to explore the risks that they may take in their lives. The lesson plan given here can be used to focus on risk-taking activity in relation to a wider variety of issues such as alcohol, sex, drugs, debt, driving and so on.

Whatever the focus, an exploration of risky behaviours is a sensitive subject and students might not want to share their personal experiences in the group. A good discussion can take place without personal disclosure if situations are provided by the teacher, printed on cards and used as a basis of discussion. The examples can be fictitious or taken from newspapers and the media. You can always have blank cards so that students can add their own examples as they feel more comfortable and confident in the group.

Learning outcomes
Students:

▶ know the risks attached to some activities which young people are prepared to do
▶ decide which risks are acceptable to them
▶ consider how to protect themselves and stay safe.

Beginning phase
Remind the students of the groundrules for discussion of sensitive or confidential issues.

G *Games*
Play Silent Statements using the sentence stem 'Cross the circle if you ...' to raise a range of risky behaviours or activities.

Cross the circle if you ...

> ⇨ have ever come home later than you were allowed.
> ⇨ have ever lied about where you were going.
> ⇨ have asked for a half-fare when you should have paid full price.
> ⇨ have drunk alcohol in a pub under age.
> ⇨ have ever broken the speed limit.

Play Sixes without and then with Guardian Angels to show that we can protect people.

Middle phase
(G) *Game*

Play Line Up! Ask the students to stand and move to a place on a line that cuts across the room. One end represents 'high risk' and the other end represents 'low risk'. Give them a statement and ask them to place themselves on the line according to how risky they think the activity is.

Risky activities

⇨ Walking home alone at 2. a.m.
⇨ Leaving a drink unattended in a nightclub.
⇨ Smoking the occasional cigarette.
⇨ Having unprotected sex.
⇨ Smoking cannabis.
⇨ Riding a bike without a crash helmet.
⇨ Drinking and driving.
⇨ Drinking more than 14–21 units of alcohol a week.
⇨ Having a body piercing or tattoo.
⇨ Leaving a party with someone you have just met.

Pairs

Give each pair one of the examples, ask them to decide on what could be done to reduce the risks of this particular activity. Pairs think of as many ways as they can to reduce the risk.

Open discussion

Take feedback in the whole circle on ways of reducing the risk of different activities. In the circle ask if anyone has known someone who has been in one of these situations. Is there a real-life story to tell? Invite the circle to offer suggestions and advice that would have reduced the harm in the story. In case no one volunteers to tell a story, make sure you have some media or personal stories to use for this activity.

Closing phase

Pairs

Put the students into pairs and ask them to produce their 'Top Ten Tips for Risk Reduction'.

Round

Finish the circle with a closing round that starts 'For my own safety I will try to ...'

Resources

- Speaking object (optional at this age and stage)
- Pens and paper
- Local or national paper for scenarios.

Section Five

Games for Circle Time

Mixing games

Often students will come into the circle and sit with their friends. The circle may have one side boys and the other side girls and some students will be deliberately excluded from groups. There are times in PSHE when we want students to work in friendship groups or pairs but this is not always the case. Good practice encourages students to work with any member of the group irrespective of friendship. Sometimes it is really useful to have a way of mixing up the group without having to say 'Please make sure that you are sat next to a member of the opposite sex'. A range of games designed to mix up the group, develop self-confidence and reveal what students are thinking is presented here.

Silent Statements

This is probably the most used game for circles because it mixes up the group and allows students to make personal statements about themselves without speaking and without pressure. This game needs to be kept fast or it can become tedious, so you may only need about five statements before moving on.

The game is played at first with the teacher leading. She turns her chair round and goes to the centre of the circle. She explains that the students need to listen carefully, then get up and cross the circle to find a new seat if the statements applies to them, for instance 'Cross the circle if you like salad'. It is important to establish a few simple, sensible rules from the students before you start, such as Walk, No touching, No noise. This should avoid chaos!

It is easy to start by choosing obvious things like 'Cross the circle if you have blue eyes/are wearing a sweatshirt/like coffee', and then progress to more personal statements such as 'Cross the circle if you cleaned your teeth this morning'. The statements can be designed to match the theme of the lesson. For instance, a Healthy Eating circle could start with non-threatening statements like 'Cross the circle if you like salad/drink water/prefer Coke to cake . . .' and progress to 'Cross the circle if you had a cooked meal last night/think eating crisps is OK/think that fashion models are too skinny'. Once you feel you can trust the group, the teacher can sit down after the first few statements to allow a student to stay in the centre and choose a statement. The ideal is where the teacher is facilitator and equal rather than controller. If you want every statement to fit the theme, you can write statements on cards and have them ready to hand to the student in the centre if they cannot think of their own. Each student usually only has one go in the centre. Any student who deliberately hovers in the middle will be asked to give their turn away, so that everyone can go once. Speed up the changes by counting down '5,4,3,2..1!' to get them back to their seats fast. Some teachers prefer to have the person choosing the statement continuing to sit in the circle rather than moving into the centre. Just as with the speaking object, it's a matter of personal choice and you must adapt this to suit what feels comfortable and works for you.

If the main objective is to mix students up, keep an eye on the movement and stop when they are well-mixed. If some students seem stuck to a friend or the seat, try 'Cross the circle if you haven't moved yet!' or move onto a version of Fruit Salad to force students to move away from their friends.

Fruit Salad
This is a variation of Silent Statements. It is easy to move from Fruit Salad to Silent Statements or the other way round. This is very useful if the class are trying to stay in friendship or gender groups and seem very reluctant to split from each other. Decide on an appropriate theme. The game is known as Fruit Salad because the original

categories were 'Apple, Orange, Banana'. Go round the group giving each student one of the three fruits in turn. Sometimes it helps to make them adopt a silly pose to help them remember their fruit. Ask the first students what they'd suggest as an *aide-mémoire*. You may have all the apples with a finger poking out of their heads to be a stalk; the oranges could hold their arms out in a circle shape and so on. Once everyone has been allocated a category (don't forget yourself) remind the group of the rules. Explain that when a fruit is called, only those people move. If someone calls 'Fruit Bowl', everyone moves. Then start by calling one of the fruits. Watch to check that all the bananas *are* actually moving. You may want to keep control the first few times you play the game, then let the students choose. Inevitably there will be the needy student who hangs around in the middle, not 'seeing' the space so she can have the centre stage. If this happens, do a count down – 'Five, four, three, two, one' – and they should all move faster to their seats. If a student has already had a go, insist that she kindly gives her go to someone else and then praise her for doing so. Always end on a fruit so that students do not have free choice about where to sit. Keep an eye on your difficult students and make sure they are split up before continuing to move into the next game or phase of the lesson.

Variations to this game are endless. If you are running a lesson on Friendship, you could take characters from a story or novel the students have read or a film they have seen recently and use these as your categories. For 11-year-olds *The Simpsons* is usually popular. Bart, Maggie and Homer are named and can sit in suitable poses chosen by the students. The students will usually come up with the ideas and 'own' them much better than if you give them the categories or ideas. Always take every opportunity to make links and connections with the theme of the lesson. For instance, a lesson on Drugs may have students choosing drug names as categories such as 'Cocaine', 'Alcohol', 'Cannabis'.

Games for beginning and closing phases

Name Chain
This is a great game for learning new names and is perfect for new groups to get to know each other or even for parents'

evenings! The facilitator starts by saying, 'My name is Miss Jones'. The first student to her right says 'This is Miss Jones and my name is John' and so on round the circle. This can be used in many different ways.

Alliterative Adjectives

This is another great fun game for learning names to bond a group. Everyone thinks of an alliterative adjective to describe themselves positively, such as 'I am Bike-mad Ben'. To help them remember the names you can ask them to add a movement to echo the adjective, which adds to the silliness and fun. Students can repeat each name adjective and movement as they to round the circle, or just repeat their neighbour's – you can adjust the game to the group though it motivates students if they know they will receive a reward if they remember all the names in a class or group.

Name games are important for all year groups. Our research showed that many 14-year-old students felt uncomfortable with new peers and needed some kind of 'getting to know you' activity before they felt calm and safe enough to concentrate in the new group.

All About You

A variation or progression of the Name Chain game is to pair students up. Always make sure that you do this rather than leaving it to the students to choose pairs. Quickly go round the circle and physically point to the neighbouring pairs you want. That way you can check who is paired with whom, possibly making a few judicious swaps if you need to.

Once in pairs, students have two minutes to find out three facts about their partner. The more interesting or bizarre the better. You may need to remind them to swap over so both have an equal chance to speak! Then they go round the circle introducing the partners. 'This is Azim. He likes hard boiled eggs, has four terrapins and has broken his arm three times'. The trick is to move fast to keep the pace up, then check for good listening by asking, 'Hands up if you know two facts about Chantelle' or 'Who can tell me the names of students who have broken their arms?' and so on. Of course, you can choose the topics you wish depending on the lesson plan and the points you want to draw out.

Up Down Up

Everyone in the circle has to stand then sit whenever they hear their name called. The facilitator says the name of the person to his right, his own name, then the name of the person on his left: 'This is Terry, I am Mr Rose and this is Mustapha'. As soon as the facilitator says, 'This is Terry', he stands up and sits down again. At the mention of his own name, the facilitator stands up and sits down and then Mustapha does the same. As soon as Mustapha has sat down, it is his turn to say, 'That is Mr Rose, I am Mustapha and this is Serena'. Mr Rose stands and sits, followed by Mustapha and then Serena. Serena repeats this pattern and so on round the circle. The game is best played quite fast so that people are standing up and sitting down in rapid succession. This game is even more fun if there are several students with the same name in the group. If their name is called, even if does not refer to them, they must stand and then sit down again when they hear their name.

Bottle Swap

Have an empty plastic soft drink bottle washed out, with the lid on tight! If the floor is very slippery, it is a good idea to make a mark on the floor with chalk, dry-wipe felt-tip or even use a mouse mat so the bottle stays central. Two students volunteer and their chairs are turned around out of play. One student stands in the centre of the circle and spins the bottle gently. The other volunteer is outside the circle. There has to be enough room for the person outside the circle to get into the circle between the chairs. The central student spins the bottle. When it stops, the central student calls the names of the two students the ends of the bottle point to. They have to swap places. The outside volunteer cannot move until the bottle stops spinning and the names have been called, but then has to run into the circle and take a chair that one of the pair vacated. The game can become confused if students cannot see clearly who the bottle points to so it is important that the spinner calls out the names of the students who are to move. The displaced person becomes the spinner and the spinner becomes the outside runner. If the group find the game hard, it can be played without the person on the outside of the circle until the chaos reduces!

Link Up

This is a good game for a group or tutor set who do not know each other well or who need to loosen up. They all stand. You explain that you will call out numbers at random. In silence, they have 15 seconds to find that number of students and link arms with them. (If you call 'Two' then two students must link arms; if 'Five', then five students link arms and so on.) It helps to demonstrate the game by using a few volunteers. Once a group is formed, they raise their linked arms together. It is vital that you act as facilitator to help out uneven groups. Explain that you can be any number they need to make up the last group. That way no group should be too stuck.

This game takes some time to get the hang of. Success depends on how fast you play it so there is no room for refusal to link arms with particular students. If necessary, you can award points for speed of response and praise those who are willing to swap groups for the sake of others. Silence is essential in order to keep control as there is a strict time limit. Any very reluctant students can be observers to watch for those students who co-operated well. They can report back at the end, but must stay positive and remember the rule that nobody can use anybody else's name negatively. This is a great way of praising the way the group gradually starts to co-operate.

Link Up leads nicely into a round about working together, co-operation, teamwork or some work on Citizenship. Asking what made the game work best is a great way to encourage reflective thinking, the need for co-operation and the ability to move away from friends for the sake of the game. More mature, experienced groups can extend their thinking into self-evaluation about how well they played and what they learned about themselves and each other. Team roles can also be explored.

Rocket Launch!

This is a game for strengthening observation skills and co-operation. You explain that the group must be aware of their body language and unspoken signals. They must co-operate to work as a team in order to get to the end. Basically, you need to know how many students there are in the group. Once you have said 'Go!' members of the group stand up and shout numbers in turn, one at a time. If there were 29 students, the first person will need to look round, stand up and start with the shout '29' and stay standing. Then the next person needs to check they are OK to go next by observing the body language of the group, stand and shout '28' and so on. If they get to 'One', then everyone shouts 'Rocket Launch!' or makes suitable noises to show the countdown has worked. If two people stand and shout the same number at the same time, everyone has to sit down and the count down starts again. Usually the more egotistical members will start by standing and shouting out without any care for the others. They soon realise that this stops the game working. You can use any mistakes to open a discussion about what helps to make the game work.

Gradually the students get the hang of it and by the end of a term's practice, you should be able to get the whole group to count down all the way to zero from thirty or however many students there are in the group. Difficult groups can even be videoed at the start and end of a term to show how much better they are at working together. The game only takes a few minutes and can lead to extended work on body language, noticing signs in people or 'reading' signals, as well as the importance of working together.

Four Up
This is a variation of Rocket Launch! which also tests a group's co-operation skills. It is good for improving group cohesion and co-operation. The game starts with a full circle of chairs. You ask for four volunteers, explaining that there must be four people in the middle of the circle at any one time. The only rule is that nobody can stay for more than ten seconds and everyone must have a go. Start with the first four people. They come and stand in the centre of the circle, facing each corner of the room. They can choose to stay for a count of ten or sit back in their place after two or three seconds. Whatever happens, they must be 'rescued' by someone else volunteering to go to the centre. At first some students will go up lots of times, but gradually everyone goes up after a while. It is good to

get the group to see how they can help each other out by standing up or by sitting down again if too many people want a go and so on. It only takes a minute or so, but can be done well and in silence producing plenty of praise from the facilitator.

Of course, you can ring the changes by having one of the people sitting, one standing on one leg, one kneeling and so on as they become more adept. To check who goes up, you can introduce a rule that people who have been up sit with their arms or legs crossed and the game stops when everyone has their legs crossed.

Catch It!
This is where you have the central volunteer throwing a ball, bean bag or duster up into the air as high as safely possible and calling a name. The named person must dash into the centre to catch the ball, bean bag or duster. If she catches it, she gets the next turn of throwing the object and calling the name of the catcher. If she fails to catch it, the original thrower has another turn. The success of this game depends very much on the skill of the thrower, the fitness of the group, the height of the ceiling and how settled the group is. It is essential that the fair play element of the game is emphasised by explaining that more than two no-throws (too high, outside the circle and so on) means that the central person has lost the turn. A room with a high ceiling is useful for this game.

Paper Plates
This is a quieter game using paper or plastic plates. Place one paper plate on each person's head. The students may have to get used to balancing it. Then, at your command, various individuals or groups have to cross the circle keeping the plate balanced on their head without using their hands. If it falls off, the student must stand stock still until a student crossing the circle replaces the plate, without letting her own plate fall off her head! You can gradually extend the number of students crossing the circle as they get used to the rules and become better at balancing the plates. Again you can play this in silence if you want a calm, controlled group! It helps to write numbers on the plates when a class first plays this game. You can then call out two numbers who swap places before extending the

game to include several numbers. Once the game is established, you can use categories of students to cross the circle such as all those with blue eyes and so on.

Bouncing Ball (or Bean Bag)

This uses the paper or plastic plates again. Everyone has a plate. You start by bouncing a soft ball, possibly a foam juggling or tennis ball, round the circle to each student in turn. Once the students are familiar with the way the ball bounces and can send it sensibly round the circle, the ball is bounced by the first person and caught on a plate by the second person. He then bounces it carefully by dropping it off his plate so his next-door neighbour can catch it on her plate. This can be done quite quietly. Students who bounce the ball wildly will stop the ball going round the circle so you may need to stop the game to discuss what is happening and encourage them to co-operate. If the group skills are not very good, it helps to substitute a bean bag for the ball and throw it very gently from plate to plate. The game can be varied or extended by increasing the number of balls or bean bags being passed at the same time. It is easier if they go round in the same direction, but two in the opposite direction creates an interesting challenge when they cross over. Another variation is to use coloured plates so that only those with red plates or blue ones can throw or catch the ball. Or you can use students' names or characteristics such as 'people wearing sweatshirts' so only selected students can throw or catch the ball at any one time. If you worry that chaos will result from playing this game, restrict it to one or two objects going in the same direction from plate to plate, with students staying on or at least touching their chairs to avoid a free for all. Using balloons instead of balls slows the game down, but can be frustrating because they tend to drift off, causing students to chase after them away from their seats.

Once you start playing this sort of game regularly, not only does your own confidence grow, but the students will increasingly 'own' the activities. If you are stumped for a game or new variation, they will often come up with suggestions and ideas of their own. Some groups even run their own sessions or you can ask particular students to run the opening or closing games. Quite a few secondary schools now have 17- and 18- year-olds running circles for the students who are new to the school.

Knee Tapping

This is a game for classes you know well! Everyone sits very close together with their knees slightly apart. They then place their right hand on the right knee of the person on their right and their left hand on the left knee of the person on their left. The idea is to tap the knees in order round the circle. This means that different people's hands have to tap one after another. Decide which knee forms the start and pass the taps on trying to build up speed. Once this is established in one direction, introduce a double tap which changes the direction the tap travels round the circle. This game can be hilarious!

If you have a group that feels unsafe using knees, a variation is to use the floor. The group members kneel on the floor in a circle. They place their left hand palm down on the floor to the left of the right hand of the person to their left (the arms cross over one another). They do the same with their right hand, placing it palm down on the floor to the right of the left hand of the person on their right. In this way, the hands alternate round the circle. Someone starts and taps the floor with his hand. The next hand round the circle then taps the floor and so on until the tap has gone right round the circle. Once the game is established, a double tap can be introduced. When someone taps the floor twice, the direction is reversed and the tap travels round the circle in the opposite direction. This game can be very funny and is excellent for quiet concentration at the end of a circle or a lesson. It can be done on table tops if students are sat round tables or desks such as in technology or science.

No Laughing Matter!

In this game students take turns in trying to make people laugh. There are many variations. One is where the volunteer goes up to each student in turn and says, in whatever manner she likes, 'I love you, baby, but I just can't smile!' If the student smiles or laughs, the volunteer moves on and tries to make someone else laugh. If the volunteer laughs or the student stays serious, then they swap places.

Another variation is where the volunteer asks each student in turn a question, to which the answer must always be the same word, for example 'Elephants'. The volunteer may ask, 'What are your bones made of?' The other person replies 'Elephants' and so the game goes on. This is a good ice-breaker and a great way to relieve tension or gel a group that seems awkward with each other.

Wink Sleep

This game has often been called Wink Murder. Choose two 'detectives' who go out of the room. While they are out of sight and earshot, you choose a volunteer who is the 'Sleep maker'. The volunteer puts people to sleep by catching their eye and winking at them. When the detectives return they watch the group and try to work out who is sending the students to sleep by winking at them. Students must be honest about their part in the game. They can't avoid eye contact to avoid being put to sleep and if the volunteer winks at them they must go to sleep. It also helps if students go to sleep quietly. If the students have played Wink Murder before, they can seriously disrupt the lesson by dramatic 'deaths' which, though hilarious, can take up too much time and become disruptive!

Racing Pictionary

This is a fast team game which is great fun and can be used for revision of key words or to expose stereotypes. You make a list of between 10 and 20 items as diverse as 'Eiffel Tower' to 'Bugs Bunny'. Divide the class into groups of four or five students. Each group has one pencil and paper block and moves to an area of the room where they are separate and can't see what another group is doing. It may help to have a desk that they sit round away from other groups, or they can sit round a chair and use the seat of the chair as a desk. One student from each group holds the pencil and comes up to the teacher. You whisper the first word from the list to them and they rush off to draw it for their group. No writing or hand gestures can be used and no words can be spoken by the drawer. When the students in a group guess what the drawing is, they must whisper so the other teams don't hear. Once somebody in the group guesses correctly, he takes the pencil, rushes up to the teacher and whispers the answer. If the answer is correct, the teacher whispers the next clue to him and so on down the list. Beware of cheats. You can challenge the team member and ask to see the drawing if you suspect cheating and any student who really dislikes this game could be used as an observer to keep an eye on fair play. The winning team is the one that guesses all the items on the teacher's list first.

This game can be adapted for use with revision lists in any subject or to introduce a discussion in PSHE or Citizenship which involves an exploration of stereotypes. It helps if the list starts with easy clues and then moves on to harder ones. A random list could include any items such as: tea bag; London Eye; Shakespeare; Shetland pony; Manchester United; McDonald's; cheeseburger; *Panorama*; cutting edge; and so on.

What's Changed?
This game is about using close observation to notice small differences. Before the game begins, the students need to look very carefully at everyone in the group. Some people might find this a bit embarrassing, so remember to stress the groundrule that says no negative comments are allowed. Ask for two volunteers who have to talk to one another in order to play the game. Co-operation is the key to playing this game successfully, so we often choose two students, possibly a boy and a girl, who may not get on that well so that they have to practise their co-operation skills. The two chosen volunteers go out of the room while everyone changes something about their appearance. When you first play this game, it is best to change just one thing each or to select a few people who change one thing. As the group becomes more skilled at observation, each person in the group can change two or even three things about their appearance. They may remove a tie, take a shoe off, roll up their sleeves, take their glasses off or put them on upside down and so on. When everyone is ready they all sit silent and demure while the 'detectives' return. The detectives walk round the circle together and between them decide what has changed for each person. They state it loudly and move on. If you need the game to move faster, you can have the class all standing still, with the detectives moving round separately. The students sit down and adjust their changes back to normal once their 'change' has been

correctly identified. This saves time at the end when they have to find their shoes, jumpers, ties and so on. There are usually one or two left at the end who have made a subtle change that is perfectly clear to everyone except the poor detectives. This can lead to quite a lot of harmless fun since everyone else knows. If the detectives are stuck, a few hints can help them to find the change such as waving an arm or pointing to the area of change. A variation for less skilled groups may be that the pair leaves the room and they change something about themselves. On their return, every student must look and decide what it is they have changed. They can put their hand up or fold their arms when they know. Some students may still need some hints, but this can speed up the game if it has slowed down too much.

Where's the Object?

This is really simple, but can be a game for the closing phase of Circle Time that gives the group a 'feel good' factor. One or two 'detectives' go out while either the teacher or someone in the class hides an agreed object somewhere in the room. At your signal the detectives return and try to find the object. The class guides the search by humming. The volume of hum indicates how close they are to the object. A soft hum means far away and increasing the volume of humming indicates that the detectives are getting closer. If humming is inappropriate for any reason, the game can be played by nodding and shaking heads. The game ends when the detectives discover the hidden object.

Adverbs

This is good for extending students' emotional vocabulary as recommended in the social, emotional and behavioural skills (SEBS) programme. It is particularly useful for developing a vocabulary to talk about moods and gradation of emotions. Two 'detectives' leave the room while the group decides on an appropriate adverb. It could be a simple one to start with, like 'slowly', and move on to more sophisticated ones such as 'passionately'. When the detectives return they ask the whole class to do an action in this manner. Instead of just one poor student having to clean her teeth 'aggressively', the whole class has to do it. It is easier to get everyone involved this way and because they are not centre stage most students, even shy ones, usually take part with increasing enjoyment and confidence. The detectives can ask for three actions and have three guesses before the game moves on. The class decides how generous they will be with clues. It is helpful to check the class's understanding of the adverb chosen before they mime it, especially with lower ability groups.

Guess the Rule

This is an excellent thinking game which can be debriefed in an open discussion to decide which strategies work best. Two 'detectives' go out of the room and the group has to think of a simple rule they will obey when the detectives return. It may be that everyone with brown eyes refuses to answer. It may be that all the boys answer 'sausages!' to any question. It could be that anyone with a collar showing refuses to reply, or lies. The permutations are endless.

Once the group has agreed on a rule, it must be crystal clear to everyone. It may need the facilitator's firm hand and skill to ensure that everyone understands. Then the detectives return. They have to move round the circle asking people the same question in turn. They can work together or if you need the game to progress faster, they can work separately and then confer. They can ask questions like 'What is your name?', 'Is this a science lesson?', 'Do you eat school dinners?' and so on. They receive various replies and use the evidence to work out why people answer in particular ways. They will need to collaborate and there is some (hilarious) pressure, since the whole class, except the detectives, knows the rule. It helps if you have fairly simple rules when you first play this game such as 'Boys tell the truth and girls lie' and you may need to do a bit of judicious pairing, supporting or suggesting at first. For instance, you could get everyone who lied or would not answer to stand up so they are more obvious and so make the rule clearer. Some groups of students aged 16 and 17 become very sophisticated and subtle, using things like crossed legs or arms or the number of syllables in the question to change the responses. For less experienced groups keep an eye out for the 'helpful friend' who is mouthing or pointing to the answer to help their classmate.

Ring on a String

Thread a smallish curtain ring (small brass ones are best) onto a long piece of soft string. Parcel string is good as garden string can burn the hands. Join the string up into a loop which is large enough to go round the whole circle with everyone holding it with both hands. One person volunteers to be the 'detective' and leaves the room or closes his eyes. While he is unable to see, the ring is passed round the circle on the string under people's hands. When the teacher shouts 'Stop!' everyone freezes and the detective comes back into the centre of the circle and tries to guess who has the ring concealed in their hand. Variations can be worked where students move the ring while the detective watches or even do without the string. Another variation is to pass the speaking object from person to person with their hands behind their backs. This game can lead on to a discussion about lie detecting, body language and guilt!

Games to refocus attention

These can be used in any lesson time as well as in Circle Time. They stop the teacher having to shout and can enliven the class and refocus students' attention before things get out of hand. Most students need to move or have some sort of kinaesthetic change after about 20 minutes. Having a variety of activities up your sleeve to grab attention can help maintain concentration and a pleasant atmosphere in your class. Of course, the students inevitably ask for another go or a further game. Get round that by saying, 'Of course we can play another, once we've finished the work'. Then point to the board with the lesson objectives on and specify how much of the lesson the group has to have done before you can play another game at the end.

All Change

Everyone folds their arms apart from the leader. Pupils have to watch the leader do an action such as brushing her hair, patting her stomach, touching alternate elbows and so on. The leader then calls 'Change' and changes her action. The rest of the class have to do the action that she was doing before calling 'Change'. This takes great concentration as they are receiving a visual input yet having to recall the last action and kinaesthetically reproduce it. The game continues with the action changing every 30 seconds or so until the leader runs out of ideas and folds her arms to indicate the game has ended after she says the last 'Change!' at the end.

This is a great game for concentration skills and is a form of 'brain gym'. You may have to watch for mischievous pupils making crazy moves. It's quite fun to make faces, but not much fun being made to jump up and down on one leg for ages. Variations of this game such as Member of the Orchestra require the leader to mime playing different instruments. As she says 'Change', the class mime the previous musical instrument as she goes on to a new one.

Aliens

This can go down well with older, 'cool' students once they know it's sometimes used as an adult or pub drinking game! One person calls a classmate's name. That person has to put up two 'antennae' on his head using his index fingers. The people either side of him have to put up one antenna each with the index finger nearest him. The person with two 'antennae' or fingers on his head calls another name. The named person immediately puts up her fingers to make antennae and the two people either side of her have one antenna each using the hand closest to her. When students have had a turn, they cross their feet to show that they have been called and can't be called again. The game is best played as fast as possible. It is great for concentration and can be used in circle sessions or in a lesson if the students are going off task. The point is to go so fast that you catch students day-dreaming so they don't put their antennae up and have to be prompted. This can be hilarious but needs to be fast-moving. The group needs to be quiet so they can hear the name being called.

Silent Aliens

A more sophisticated version of Aliens is where the alien points in silence to their chosen person using eye contact and antennae pointing only. It is important that the correct person is identified. This can be confirmed by lots of head shaking or goofy antennae waggling.

Rabbit's Ears

This game is identical to Aliens except the person whose name is called uses two hands to make rabbits' ears on either side of his head. The people sat either side of him have to put up one ear each with the hand nearest to the person who was called. The named person sends the rabbit's ears to another person by calling out his or her name and then crosses her legs to show that she has already had a turn.

Racing Cars

It is best to demonstrate this game yourself. Explain that it needs to be done fast and dramatically and everyone must stay alert. You turn your head fast to look at the person next to you. You can go either way round the circle and as you turn your head you say, 'Zoom!' Your neighbour does the same instantly so the Zoom is passed round the circle like a racing car with heads turning fast. Once it's gone all the way round to you again, you stop it with an 'eek' which sounds like the squealing of brakes. You explain that eeks are very powerful because anyone who eeks can alter the direction of the Zoom. At first you may only give out a few eeks, possibly even on cards so they can only be used once. Later everyone can have just one eek and cross their legs or arms once it has been used up. When everyone has an eek to use, you will find that the students want to use their eeks and the game will get stuck in one section of the circle with the Zoom going backwards and forwards within a sector. The students are just having fun. It always happens, but the problem is that some people will get left out of the game as a result. This becomes a superb opportunity to talk about leaving people out, how it feels to be isolated or to be the people in the 'in' group. In the game, people tend to get mildly annoyed if they miss a turn but the emotions are similar to the stronger ones that they feel when they are left out in real-life situations. The game and its associated feelings are a perfect way to start a discussion about the issues of power, inclusion, exclusion, control and powerlessness.

As well as being a good game for encouraging quick concentration, it's fun and a great way to end a lesson because you can send the 'car' round the classroom. It is fast and only takes a minute. A further variation is passing a tapped or clapped rhythm round the group just at the end of the lesson. Once they have clapped their rhythm they can stand and move to the door or pack up.

Bing, Bang, Boing!
This is a variation of Racing Cars with more alternatives. Basically, the leader puts his hands together with the palms facing one another and points his fingers at the person to his left saying, 'Bing'. The receiver can choose to continue in the same direction by pointing to her left and calling 'Bing' or she could choose to send the action the other way by pointing to the right and saying 'Bang'. Every five moves, the person who has the turn can choose to send it across the circle by calling 'Boing' and pointing to someone on the other side of the room. This keeps everyone on their toes and can be very funny. Hopefully anyone caught napping will laugh it off, and be sure to keep on the ball later! It is vital that 'Boings' across the circle are clearly caught and passed on so that no confusion arises with two people passing 'Bings'. One way to get over this is to make the sender call the name as well as 'Boing'. For example, 'Boing Catherine!' makes it clear who the 'Boing' is going to.

Sixes
This is another group co-operation game where you must be careful that the group do not gang up on anyone. The idea is that everyone starts by standing up. They then count in turn round the circle. Each person can choose to say one, two or three numbers, but every time the count gets to six that person 'dies' and has to sit down. So the teacher may start by saying, 'one'. The next person might say 'two, three', the next person could say 'four, five' and the next person quietly says 'six' crosses his arms and sits down. He is left out for the rest of the game. The game should be played very fast so that those who are out early on do not get bored and very soon only a couple of students are left standing. If you have a group that tries to get each other out or gangs up on some less popular students, you can have 'Guardian Angels'.

Sixes with Guardian Angels

Guardian Angels are the students who are either side of the people who may be vulnerable during Sixes. The Guardian Angels become heroes who volunteer to sacrifice themselves rather than let the people they are protecting die. This can lead to interesting discussions about supporting or protecting others and being a good citizen.

Mexican Wave

Another game to enhance group cohesion is passing an action like a wave round the circle. It is passed by standing up and putting your hands into the air. As soon as you sit down, the next person on your right begins to stand up and so it follows on smoothly. Once it's gone all the way round you can change the action so that everyone copies, aiming for good observation, concentration and a smooth passing round. This usually brings in the reluctant students as they ruin the effect if they sit with folded arms refusing to join in. If you have the bulk of the class with you, reluctant ones will be very unpopular if they spoil it for the others. If they resolutely refuse, let the wave (or any game) pass over them and move on quickly without fuss.

Chinese Whispers

In this game a simple, short message is whispered from person to person round the circle. The idea is that as the message is passed from one person to the next, excellent communication skills will mean the message comes out unadulterated. Sometimes the message is deliberately sabotaged and it helps to debrief the game by going round the circle to find out where the message changed. The game can be played again to see if it can be completed without any silly behaviour. If you are afraid that the group will misbehave, write down some simple phrases on a card to show the person starting the round. Any student who is stuck can be shown the card to keep the round going. In weaker groups, make the sentence very short and simple. As the group becomes more skilled, the sentence can become longer and more complex.

132

Line Up!

This is a useful activity to sort out or mix up students quickly. Basically, you ask them to get into a line along a continuum which has one extreme at one end and the opposite extreme at the other end. Continuum lines could be shoe sizes with size 1 at one end and size 15 at the other end. Students place themselves on the line where their shoe size would fall. The ends of the line could be 'Strongly agree' at one end and 'Strongly disagree' at the other end. The class are then presented with controversial statements such as 'All animal experimentation is wrong' and they have to stand on the part of the line which most accurately reflects the strength of their feeling.

Other forms of line up can be used in the circle as a PSHE activity. The students can be asked to line up silently in order of their ages, in alphabetical order of last names or alphabetical order of first names and so on. It is very useful to line up tutor sets in the five or so minutes while waiting to be called for assembly or for the bell to go. It is also fun for a teaching group that seems a bit dull to liven up by making themselves physically move to express their opinion and become more active participants in the learning. It is useful to note that large groups may have to line up round the circle or you may want to make a space either side of the circle so that the line can extend through it.

Who's the Leader?

This is another detective game. Send one or two 'detectives' out and ask for a volunteer in the group whose job it is to lead an action. Actions can include tapping knees or shoulders, waving hands in the air, touching feet and so on. The leader chooses an action and starts the group off before the detectives return, then she changes the action quite frequently and as subtly as possible. The detectives must watch to see who is leading the changes. Many variations can be used to make the game easier or harder, depending on the group. If they are stuck for ideas, ask them to mime jobs or instruments to play. After three guesses change the leader and detectives to keep the pace fast.

I Packed My Bag

This is a time-honoured game for increasing concentration. One student starts by saying, 'I packed my bag for school (or whatever you are covering in the lesson) and in it I put my sandwiches'. The next student repeats the phrase but adds an item such as, 'I packed my bag for school and in it I put my sandwiches and my planner'. This continues round the circle until somebody forgets or goes wrong. A game such as I Packed My Bag is useful for recalling key words during revision. It can be used for French verbs, major historical dates, enzymes and so on. For instance, 'I ate a sandwich and my digestive system produced ptyalin'. It can also help with organisational skills as in the script for 14-to 15-year-olds on work experience preparation (page 90) where students have to work out what to take with them. There are many variations for the introductory phrase, including 'I went shopping and I bought . . .', 'If I had £20 to spend I'd buy . . .' and so on.

Excuse Me

This is an amusing game that requires observation and concentration but gives rise to a lot of laughter and fun. It begins with a student miming an action such as cleaning his shoes. The next person in the circle says, 'Excuse me, what are you doing?' The first student, still miming cleaning his shoes, says, 'Oh, I'm riding my bike'. The second student, the one who asked the question, must now mime riding a bike. The next student round the circle then asks the second one, 'Excuse me, what are you doing?' The student miming riding her bike says something like, 'I'm playing football' where upon the third students has to mime playing football, and so the game goes on. This game is good fun but is not recommended for students for whom English is a new or additional language, as it can be very confusing!

Resources and References

Useful websites

Bullying:www.dfes.gov.uk/bullying;www.wiredforhealth.gov.uk/standup forus

Drugs and alcohol: www.lifebytes.gov.uk; www.mindbodysoul. gov.uk

Every Child Matters: www.everychildmatters.gov.uk

www.thegrid.org.uk

www.bbc.co.uk

www.campaignforlearning.org.uk

Personal, social and health education in secondary schools, January 2005: www.ofsted.gov.uk

Personal, social and health education 2002/3 annual report on curriculum and assessment: www.qca.org.uk

www.antidote.org.uk

Pupilvoice:www.standards.dfes.gov.uk/research/themes/pupil_voice

Social, emotional and behavioural skills (SEBS): www.teachernet. gov.uk

www.wiredforhealth.gov.uk

Sleep: www.stanford.edu

The government's Five Year Strategy:www.dfes.gov.uk/publications/ 5yearstrategy

Games: www.funandgames.org; www.woodcraft.org.uk/resources; www. scoutingresources.org.uk/games-index.html

Useful books for circle games

Mosley, J. and Tew, M. (1999) *Quality Circle Time in the Secondary School*. London: Fultan.

Bliss, T. and Tetley, J. (1993) *Circle Time: A Resource Book for Infant, Junior and Secondary Schools*. Bristol: Lucky Duck Publishing.

Bliss, T. and Robinson, G. (1993) *Coming Round to Circle Time*. Bristol: Lucky Duck Publishing.

Bliss, T., Robinson, G. and Maines, B. (1995) *Developing Circle Time*. Bristol: Lucky Duck Publishing.

Smith, C. (2003a) *Introducing Circle Time to Secondary Students*. Bristol: Lucky Duck Publishing.

Smith, C. (2003b) *More Circle Time for Secondary Students*. Bristol: Lucky Duck Publishing.

Smith, C. (2003c) *Concluding Circle Time with Secondary Students*. Bristol: Lucky Duck Publishing.

Smith, C. (2004) *Circle Time for Adolescents*. Bristol: Lucky Duck Publishing.

Cavert, C., Frank, L. and Friends (1999) *Games & Other Stuff for Teachers: Classroom Activities that Promote Pro-Social Learning*. Oklahoma City, OK: Wood 'N' Barnes.

Dewar, R., Palser, K. and Notley, M. (1989) *Games, Games, Games*. London: The Woodcraft Folk.

Epstein, R. and Rogers, J. (2001) *The Big Book of Motivation Games: Quick, Fun Ways to Get People Energized*. New York: McGraw-Hill.

Jones, A. (1998) *104 Activities That Build: Self-Esteem, Teamwork, Communication, Anger Management, Self-Discovery, and Coping Skills*. Richland, WA: Rec Room Publishing.

Kroehnert, G. (1991) *Training Games*. New York: McGraw-Hill.

Newstrom, J. and Scannell, E. (1998) *The Big Book of Team Building Games: Trust-building Activities, Team Spirit Exercises, and Other Fun Things to Do*. New York: McGraw-Hill.

Tamblyn, D. and Weiss, S. (2000) *Big Book of Humorous Training Games* (Big Book of Business Games Series). New York: McGraw-Hill.

West, E. (1999) *The Big Book of Icebreakers*. New York: McGraw-Hill.

References

Bandura, A. (1997) *Self-efficacy: The Exercise of Control*. New York: W.H. Freeman and Co.

Brophy, J. (1981) 'Teacher praise: a functional analysis', *Review of Educational Research*, 51, 1, 5–32.

Burns, R. (1982) *Self-Concept Development and Education*. Dorset: Holt, Rinehart and Winston.

Canfield, J. (1990). 'Improving students' self-esteem: a focus on academic and moral values', *Educational Leadership*, 48, 48–50.

Deakin Crick, R., Broadfoot, P., Tew, M., Jelfs, H., Randall, E., Prosser, G. and Temple, S. (2004) 'The Ecology of Learning: a cross sectional exploration of relationships between learner-centred variables in five schools' http://opencreativity.open.ac.uk/recent.htm previous_papers

Goldthorpe, M. (1998) *Poems for Circle Time and Literacy Hour*. London: LDA.

Hannaford, C. (1994) *Smart Moves: Why Learning is Not All in Your Head*. Arlington, VA: Great Ocean Publishers.

Lees, J. and Plant, S. (2000) *PASSPORT – A framework for Personal and Social Development*. London: Calouste Gulbenkian Foundation.

QCA (1999) *The National Curriculum Key Stages 3 and 4*. London: QCA.

Taylor, M. J. (2003) *Going Round in Circles: Implementing and Learning from Circle Time*: Slough: NfER.

Tew, M., Deakin Crick, R., Broadfoot, P. and Claxton, G. (2004) *Learning Power: A Practitioner's Guide*. Manchester: Lifelong Learning Foundation.

Tuckman, in Napier, R. W. and Gershenfeld, M. K. (1973) *Group Theory and Experience*. Boston, MA: Houghton Mifflin.

White, M. (1991) *Self-esteem: Promoting Positive Practices for Responsible Behaviour – Circle-Time Strategies for Schools, Set A*. Cambridge: Daniels Publishing.

White, M. (1998) *Magic Circles: Building Self-esteem through Circle Time*. Bristol: Lucky Duck Publishing.

Zimbardo, P. (1969) *The Cognitive Control of Motivation: The Consequences of Choice and Dissonance*. Glenview, IL: Scott Foresman.